MICROSOFT CLOUD SECURITY FOR THE C-LEVEL

PROTECT, DETECT & RESPOND WITH AZURE CLOUD SECURITY, IN-HOUSE, IN AZURE OR IN ANY PUBLIC CLOUD.

Paul Keely MVP

Protect, Detect, and Respond.

AUDIENCE

This book is part of the C-Level Series by Paul Keely. It's a series designed to help C-Level people understand cloud security, ask the right questions and get to the business case.

This book is somewhat technical in that you will likely benefit more as the CTO, CIO or CISO than the CEO or COO for example. However, it will be presented in a way that is easy to read, to the point and well-illustrated. So, the user should have no difficulty following the content.

The chapter introduction will be high level, short and to the point. Read that and you should have enough to start a conversation. The rest of the chapter will then go deeper, but it's still at the design level. This is <u>not</u> a how-to book for the IT security administrator; rather it's for business leaders and decision makers to understand what the future vision may look like, and how to plot it.

This book will help build a framework around which you can rethink how you approach security - data-driven security.

Microsoft's future lies in the cloud, in the form of Azure. Many C-Level executives do not feel that a public cloud is a safe place for data and identities to reside. To counter this Microsoft is spending over a billion dollars a year developing a security model that is quite simply second to none. This book argues that you will, in fact be more secure by adopting a cloud-based security model.

Be prepared over the course of this book to see a solution that offers a defense in-depth, that protects your user's identities, their endpoints and the data itself. If, and when breaches occur, you will be provided with a rich suite of tools to detect that breach and remove the attacker.

INTRODUCTION

While writing this book, I was working with the Microsoft team out of mid-Atlantic. We were working with a company that was attacked with a ransomware that resulted in losses of more than ten million dollars. It caused severe service interruptions and many career changes for the C-Level IT people involved. The attack crippled services for the organization, was on the news every hour and resulted in a serious breach of trust. I am now working with the "new" CIO, CTO and CISO…. Does it seem fair that the IT C-suite suffers the consequences when the likelihood of being compromised is so high? Fairness is not something we can help with, but what we can tell you is that inside this book is a road map to help you greatly increase your ability to protect your organization. That protection comes from Microsoft and a lot of it is in the form of security services from Azure.

Our dependency on IT has grown at a curve so steep it is nearly unimaginable. Unfortunately, so have the number of high profile hacks. We are living in a world where people's lives have become more mobile and more flexible, and they want services to follow that.

Much of our working lives involved being in a company building that had firewalls and access controls to protect our data and us. Despite this security, we were still attacked every day with viruses and Trojans, often with painful results. The advent of the cloud SaaS app has meant that more and more services and data are living outside of our corporate data centers, we are interacting with more and more customers and partners, and of course, we are producing a lot of data.

One approach is not to move to the cloud in any way, keep everything in-house. There are many reasons why you may fear the cloud and the "public" nature of it all, but this book stands on the premise that you can at least use Microsoft's cloud services to keep you a lot safer than you are today. Just to be clear when we say cloud service we are talking about a software service in Azure doing some security service for you rather than you placing your corporate data in the cloud.

Using cloud-based security services whereby you can keep all your company data in your data centers in-houses, but utilize many of the tools explained here to safeguard your identities. If you adopt the principles laid out in this book and embrace the cloud, in fact, use it as your number one starting point for security, you can make your in-house data centers and offices safer places to work. Migrating workloads to the cloud can and will make that data safer than running it on in-house datacenters.

Not every area of cloud security is covered here but we include the major pillars and give you a great foundation to build and ensure better security. We finish with a chapter on Windows 10. We know this is not a cloud technology, but there have been so many changes to Windows 10, we felt it imperative to include it in this book. 97% of company client desktops/laptops are going to be Microsoft, and most of them are moving to Windows 10.

This book is designed to make it as easy as possible to understand and consume this great security suite. When you read it our advice on the next steps are:

- Develop an end state security architecture (we would love to help you with that)

- Talk to your Microsoft Account Team for advice on

  ➤ Licensing SKU's (Ideally either Microsoft 365 Business or Enterprise)
  ➤ Potential funding from Microsoft in the form of Business Investment Funding (BIF) or Cloud Investment Funding (CIF)

In 60% of IT breaches, leaked user credentials were used to gain unlawful access to corporate resources. Identity is the new control plain and any work you do to protect the end user's identity the safer you and your organization are going to be.

MICROSOFT 365

For a very long time Microsoft sold companies software in the form of a three-year agreement called an Enterprise Agreement (EA). In the summer of 2017 they announced a new way to both purchase and engage with the tools in this book. Microsoft already had a licensed SKU called the Secure Productive Enterprise E5 (SPE–E5). This essentially gave you the rights to the full suite. Microsoft now have two SKU's, Microsoft 365 Business and Enterprise. The two new SKU's are likely how all companies will interact with the suite so we are just going to cover them here. I will add an author's note that this suite was only coming out at the time of writing so it may advance further (we also update this book on a bi-monthly basis so it should be pretty up-to-date).

Microsoft 365 Business

This solution is quite unique because it's not just a set of tools with a new license name. It is a new presentation layer around security features. In this SKU, you get the best of Windows 10, Enterprise Mobility and Security and Office 365 for the small business. This is all presented to you in a new portal wherein you can configure the new PC experience from scratch, in a set of wizard driven tools. The result will be that any employee can go buy a new laptop, enter their Azure AD user name and password, and Windows 10 AutoPilot will build out the PC, get Office and other apps deployed, secure mobile devices and protect your documents. This portal basically obfuscates the challenges around deploying the full stack in this book that requires a good deal of expertise. This tool is limited to 300 users, and you cannot use on premise Active Directory (AD), so this is a small business solution.

Microsoft 365 Enterprise

This solution basically maps to the old SKU of SPE-E5. Security reports like the Verizon report show just many attacks come in from identity fraud, and to this end you need to seriously address the risk to your user's identity. There is no single greater way to address the identity issue then to use this suite. So should I not just look at the identity parts and leave the rest? Good question but to be honest the identity parts are all powered by the mighty Microsoft Intelligent Security Graph, you will learn more about this shortly. The power of this security tool is that is collects data from around the world and uses this threat data to protect all the ways your user's identities are used, from plain old logons to conditional access. If you are an enterprise customer than the Microsoft 365 Enterprise SKU is the way to go. With this suite you get the fullest security experience possible.

HOW TO USE THIS BOOK

The Introductory page

The chapter introduction will be very succinct. You may like to read the full chapter and then just review the Introduction and the mind map before you have security meetings or presentations.

- We explain the key points in a bulleted format

We will be focusing on three areas of security:

- The user's identity (username and password)
- The devices that users are using to connect to our services
- The data that the user is working with

In each chapter, we want you to know which area we are focusing on and the distinction between the three will be explicitly denoted with one or more of the icons below.

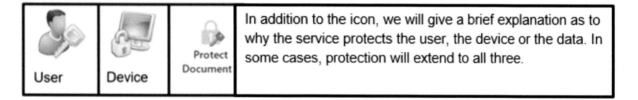

User	Device	Protect Document	In addition to the icon, we will give a brief explanation as to why the service protects the user, the device or the data. In some cases, protection will extend to all three.

The next area that we would like to draw your attention to is the location of both the service and the endpoint where the security protection is going to be applied. The following example illustrates:

Service Name	Service Location	Endpoint Location
Azure AD	Cloud	Hybrid

The service "Azure AD" is a cloud-based service from Microsoft and the endpoints like users and computers can exist in-house (Windows Active Directory) or can just exist in the cloud as Azure AD native users.

Still staying on the first page of each chapter there will be a least one QR code that you can scan on your smartphone and it will bring you to a website to watch a short video on the subject, listen to a podcast or even just bring you to a static web page, where you can just read about the topic (just read something? I know right!) This way you can get access to it quickly. If you do not have a QR code scanner just go to your app store and search a QR code scanner.

QR Code	Web location	Description
	WWW.BORNINTHECLOUD.NET	THIS IS OUR WEBSITE, A GREAT PLACE FOR PODCASTS AND BLOGS ON AZURE

The scanner that was used to test all the QR codes in this book is the QR Code Reader by Scan Inc.

QR Code Reader by Scan
Scan, Inc.
★★★★☆ (57)

OPEN

In detail

This section will elaborate on the subject and give you more resources. It will probably be useful to read the detailed section once to get a better understanding of the topic, but remember it's still at level 100 or if you are not familiar with Microsoft technical levels, it's going to be two pages max.

The project

The whole point of this book is that it gives you a high-level overview of the Microsoft security toolkit. Armed with this you will be in a better position to build out your security roadmap. In the project section, we will cover at a high-level, what the steps look like, give an estimation of the effort and complexity and arm you with what you need to make decisions on each stage.

As nearly everything covered here is a cloud based service they are not massive projects, so "quantify massive" we hear you say. Well the effort in enabling Azure AD Identity Protection would likely take no more than a few days to design, test and pilot (you are just adding a feature blade in Azure). Once successfully tested the role-out is just adding users to policies.

On the other hand, a lot of the amazing security features of Windows 10 Creator will require a client imaging project that could also involve a hardware refresh, not a trivial venture. When we say not a massive project for all the cloud-based features we are talking weeks not months. If, however you are an enormous organization with AD forest upon AD forest with hundreds of thousands of objects then everything is a pretty big deal and we are not going to tell you otherwise.

The questions

What are the key questions you need you ask your Director of IT, your Solutions Architects, and IT admins? Below are examples of some of the questions you may be asking:

- Do we have a security policy or future desired end state?
- How does ATA fit into that policy or desired end state?
- Do we have any behavior profiling software in use right now?
- What are the end-to-end costs of the project going to be?

We want this book to be useful; it's full of mind maps, diagrams, and icons to help get the point across. The QR codes give you access to the relevant web URL's from your smartphone, so you don't need to search for or type anything. This book should act as a workbook to help your team understand the challenges, the tool set and how you can use those tools to build and maintain a state of the art security stance.

The mind map

The mind map is designed to help you get a visual picture of the chapter and the book; we want this to be easy to use and reference.

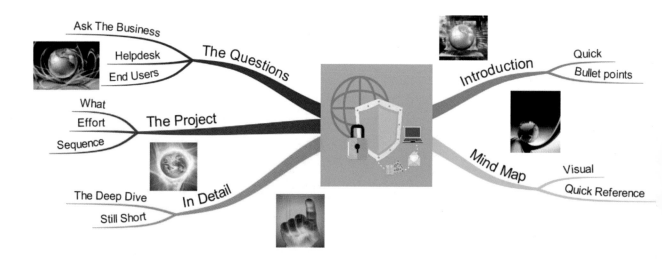

What are the problems you are trying to solve?

Q: I need to detect, and alert on unusual AD account behavior inside my network?
A: Advanced Threat Analytics is the first step, head to Chapter 2, page 23 to get started.

Q: I need post attack detection capabilities to answer 3 questions:
- Who was attacked?
- What did it do?
- Where did it go?

A: ATP is going to show you who was attacked in your environment, what the attack was and where the attack has spread to, go to Chapter 3, page 31.

Q: I have so many apps with different passwords. Password resets are killing the help desk and I need to share resources with our partners, what can I do?
A: You need to get Azure AD deployed and configured, go straight to Chapter 5, page 46.

Q: I have no idea if my users accounts are for sale. If they are compromised can I enforce higher security on them automatically?
A: This is the question on every CISO's mind. You need to get Azure AD Identity Protection deployed and configured, go straight to Chapter 6, page 54.

Q: Our Office 365 groups are full of admins, and once they get added to a group they are there forever. How can I give people access to groups only when they need it?
A: You are looking for "Just in Time" administration. You can get this with Azure AD Privileged Identity Management. Chapter 7, page 62 is the place to start.

Q: We just discovered a department is using a cloud based SaaS service. We did not approve it and we don't know if the service is reputable. Can I block a user doing a massive download?
A: The Cloud App Security Broker in Chapter 8, page 70 is the place to go.

Q: I need to protect my users with multi-factor authentication. Does Microsoft have a solution?
A: The sure do, both a cloud and in-house solutions with Phone Factor, Chapter 9, page 79 is your place to get going.

Q: We are nervous that we can't protect our data, especially when it leaves our company, what can we do?
A: Azure Information Protection will control what users are able to do with your company data. Templates that will prevent printing, forwarding and sharing will really help you get the protection you are looking for. Chapter 10, page 86 is your starting point.

Q: We have so much mobile access these days and so much of it is BYOD. How can we protect this with Microsoft's cloud?
A: Microsoft have a mobile device management solution with Intune. You may want to integrate this with SCCM and Chapter 11, page 95 is your first stop.

Q: We have resources in-house, in Azure and AWS. How can I monitor and configure these resources and know that they are secure?
A: The Operations Management Suite is the ever-evolving management suite for hybrid environments. In Chapter 12, page 102 we explore the suite.

Q: We need to secure our endpoints and the majority of them are Windows. What can I do to be as secure as possible?
A: Windows 10 Creator edition is the most secure version of Windows ever. Chapter 14, page 122 will explain why it is so secure, and what you can do to get it deployed.

Q: We have deployed a number of VM's as IaaS VM's in Azure and we know that securing those VM's is our responsibility, so is there an easy way to identify the vulnerabilities on those VM's?
A: Microsoft feel your pain and have built out an amazing tool called Azure Security Center. With this solution, you can easily identify the issues and either remediate them from inside Security Center or it will tell you how to go and perform the remediation. Chapter 13, page 113 is the place to start.

1.0 MICROSOFT'S INTELLIGENT SECURITY GRAPH

What is the problem that the Microsoft Intelligent Security Graph is trying to solve?

When attackers are rapidly changing, and adapting their attack strategies to enable them to remain undetected for long periods of time, the graph will build attack patterns on data that is global and may only be relevant for a short time period.

User	Device	Protect Document	The security graph will protect the user identity, the device and data.

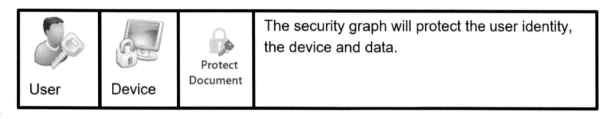

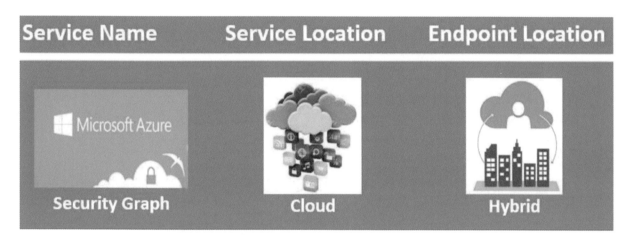

Service Name	Service Location	Endpoint Location
Microsoft Azure — Security Graph	Cloud	Hybrid

The QR code below will bring you to a video that explains the Security Graph and it's worth the 3 minutes or so it takes to watch.

QR Code	Web location	Description
	https://www.microsoft.com/en-us/security/intelligence	Describes the Intelligent Security Graph in good detail. "Billions of data points make the difference"

1.1 Introduction

Microsoft is running the largest cloud computing solutions in the world; there are literally only a handful or companies in the world on this scale. With Active Directory, Microsoft has owned authentication in-house, and have moved this knowledge to Azure. Here are some of the numbers that Microsoft are processing;

- 300+ Billion logins every month
- 1 Billion Windows devices updated
- 200 Billion emails analyzed
- 18 Billion Bing pages scanned

All these data signals from around the world are fed into the security graph. The graph allows machine learning to challenge security access and protect resources in response to threats in real time. The security rules that they change on the fly enables the graph to respond to security threats in an automated fashion.

What this means to you is:

- IP addresses and locations that were safe at one point may now be compromised, what if a user is trying to communicate from that IP?
- Unless you can challenge authentications based on near "real time" threat patterns you will lose.
- Attackers are using known safe applications, protocols and ports to attack your network. You need to be able to monitor the behavior of the file, not the file name or type.
- Microsoft's machine learning is taking billions of data points into the security graph and re-writing the rules if needed every second.
- You need to be behind that graph!

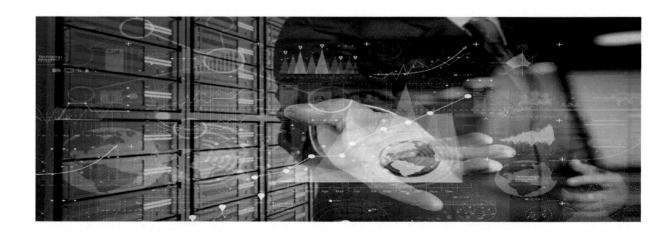

1.2 In detail

Imagine a scenario whereby one of your users gets an email from some C-Level person in the company (yes, it's spoofed, but they don't know that). The email contains a macro that they enable, and an attacker has begun an attack phase on that user. The malware in the attack in question was not picked up by your AV. However, you have deployed Windows 10, and on it there is a behavior sensor (called ATP, you will learn lots about it in chapter three) that identifies this unusual behavior, and it's sent to your ATP tenant in the cloud.

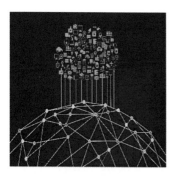

Microsoft's machine learning can pick up on this and quickly realize that it's not safe. From there the machine learning algorithms can change the filter rules in Office 365 and stop the other twenty users targeted with the same attack from getting the attachment in their inboxes.

This protection that you benefited from was just from within your organization, but now Microsoft has learned from this attack, they are identifying program hashes, patterns, and IP address and are looking to close it down and protect millions of other users.

Signals are being fed into the graph from throughout the world. This immense dataset is then being used to build profiles of IP addresses sending nefarious packets, files that are malware and login attempts that are brute forcing passwords on your user's accounts.

1.3 The project

To start using this technology and benefiting from it, there are several things you can do. Deploying Advanced Threat Protection to all your Windows 10 devices is a great start, but to really benefit from the graph you need to start brokering your authentications through Microsoft. This means you need to deploy Azure AD and make Azure AD your new identity bridge.

Microsoft's security graph can make you safer in the cloud.

It is only with the scale of the cloud that something like this graph could have ever happened. Billions of signals from around the world, being collected and analysed with machine data.

These signals result in threats from around the world being correlated and automated security responses protect your users.

1.4   The questions

- Can we build a similar solution to the security graph in-house?
- Can we protect our user's identity without using this technology?
- What are the security implications of using Azure for our company overall?
- We are heavily invested in AWS/Google/IBM cloud. Can this help us?
- What are the benefits to the business of this technology?
- What are the risks to the business of adopting the technology as a security posture?
- Have we spoken to our Microsoft account team about this technology?
- What products of our Enterprise Agreement/Microsoft 365 Enterprise that leverage the graph are we not using?
- Are other companies in our market space using this suite?

The Intelligent Security Graph

The Security Graph that Microsoft built is the first hyper scale technology concept that is going to level the playing field between you and cyber criminals.

///////////////////// Unparalleled Cloud Scale

1 Billion Windows Devices updated

300B Monthly authentications

200B Emails scanned

18+ Billion Bing web pages scanned

ADDITIONAL STATS

- Big Data can store peta bytes of data, and access it fast

- Machine learning can respond to activities that are abnormal

- Data and logs are taken from throughout the globe

//////////////////// Billions of points makes the difference

By connecting the dots between billions of people, devices and data sets the Graph can learn of a threat, rewrite rules and adapt in seconds to persistent threats.

///////////////////

The Graph monitors "Hot Spots"

Cyber criminals will capture known safe locations, and use them to commit attacks. These locations will quickly light up on the grid, and this will be used to cross reference if the communications knocking on your door are safe or not.

2.0 ADVANCED THREAT ANALYTICS (ATA)

What is the problem that ATA is trying to solve?

ATA is seeking to detect and alert you to attacks from inside your network; it will find abnormal Active Directory user account behavior, monitor it and alert you if it finds something amiss. This is the first toolset that I would deploy in my environment. I even deploy this before Azure AD.

User	Device	*While ATA's primary focus in the user account in AD, if an account has been compromised, ATA will show you the account, and then pivot to the devices the account was used on.* **This is a "Detection" tool.**

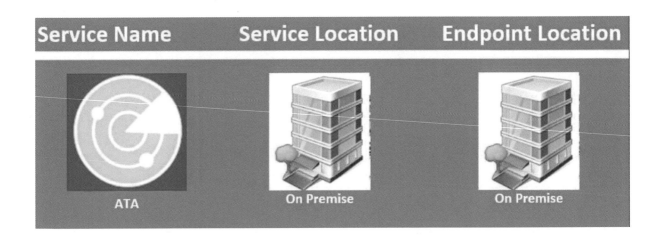

Service Name	Service Location	Endpoint Location
ATA	On Premise	On Premise

QR Code	Web location	Description
	https://www.youtube.com/watch?v=6Wz6s6onf1w&feature=youtu.be	This is a short video on ATA at the Born In The Cloud YouTube channel

2.1 Introduction

ATA is an in-house application that looks for abnormal user behavior in Active Directory. This is a book on "cloud security", this is an in-house solution for on-premises devices, so what is it doing here? This tool is an integral part of the security stance; it is part of the "new" model. In the very last chapter we also cover Windows 10, and similarly to this product, it is obviously for your on-premises environment.

This is not a complex product to install or manage and should be first on your "data driven security project list". In ATA:

- The "Center" is a dedicated server that receives the data from gateways
- The "Gateway" can be a dedicated server or a "Lightweight Gateway" installed directly onto your Domain Controllers (DC's)
- It builds a behavior pattern over time (ideally 30 days) but works straight away
- It will identify unusual activity and when it discovers behavior that is suspicious it will tell you all the users that have logged onto that machine, and all the machines that the user in question has logged onto.

In this example, you can see the "Administrator", logged onto "DESKTOP-164P" and performed a directory enumeration.

2.2 In detail

The usual authentication challenge on our internal domains consists of a username and password. Once a user successfully authenticates into our Active Directory, we don't spend any more time "profiling" that user to see if their behavior is normal. Are they doing what we expect them to do, and if not what are they doing?

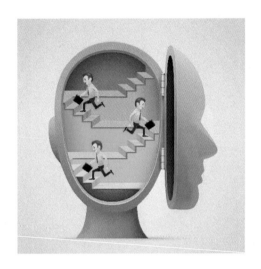

ATA looks to build out a behavior profile pattern, and when it identifies that a user has been compromised, it records where a user has been, on what machines and where a likely attacker is going. The first question you may ask is how? Aren't there thousands of different types of attacks? Yes, there are, but they all follow three stages, and it's the behavior in these three phases that ATA is looking for.

When we take a typical use case of a user, enabling a macro or downloading something dangerous through email, a three-phased approach is taken once the initial payload has been delivered. The attacker starts with a stored hash attack on the compromised device. They then start a "Reconnaissance" phase, trying to learn anything useful about your environment. They are trying to find out your IP addressing, your DC's, default gateway etc. At this phase a Pass-the-Hash style attack may be used to move to machines with other user accounts, usually referred to as "Lateral Movement". When on a high-value target, they will then move onto the last phase of "Dominance".

ATA is easy to install, requires almost no configuration, and has no tuning, that should mean that you will be up and running fast. This speed to install, lack of configuration and ease of administration means that you will get a quick return on investment (ROI) and add your first new layer of security to your environment. To install and benefit from ATA you do not need Azure Active Directory (AAD). This is one of the few tools we will be covering that is fully in-house with no cloud integration whatsoever, except that it can connect with cloud monitoring like OMS (OMS is covered later in Chapter 12).

One important consideration with this tool is that there is a small likelihood that when you deploy ATA you could find an intruder has already gained access to your network and you are under attack right now. You need to discuss what you are going to do if that is indeed the case. Who will you contact for help? Do you need to change admin passwords, remove people from groups etc. How will this be communicated and executed?

What if you already have an intrusion detection system in place, will installing ATA not just be like installing two antivirus solutions? Well to some degree this is true, but typically IDS operate on the network layer rather than at the DC layer. ATA looks at behavior and builds a profile of that behavior over time; it's not an AV's binary Yes or NO question. I would recommend deploying ATA and comparing it to your other system.

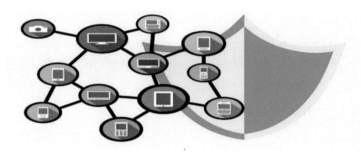

In ATA, we can look at any user or device and quickly review things like "Directory Changes", in this screen shot you can see password changes on the machine account.

DC1

Windows Server 2016 Standard, 10.0 (14393)

bitc.local
Created on Jan 24, 2017

Ⓢ Sensitive   1 suspicious activity   1 Medium

About	Account Info	Suspicious activities	Directory Changes

4:17 PM
Friday   🔘   DC1's password was changed
February 24, 2017

1:35 PM
Tuesday   🔘   DC1's password was changed
January 24, 2017

2.3 The project

How long it takes to deploy ATA, and the associated effort obviously depends on many different components and I am trying to give you some idea here of what the likely effort is compared to other projects.

ATA has three roles;

1. The Center - this is the brains of the solution and it acts as the collector from the gateways.
2. A Gateway - this role is deployed to a VM and uses port mirroring to get your DC's to send information to it.
3. A Lightweight Gateway - this role is deployed directly to your DC (every DC) and it sends information to the center (you only need to deploy either a gateway or a lightweight gateway).

The project to deploy ATA depends on your domain structure. You can only have one ATA environment per forest. ATA consists of at least one VM for the center and you could, in theory, deploy all lightweight gateways to your DC's.

Some points for the project;

- You need a dedicated VM for the "Center".
- You could just use lightweight gateways on your DC's and not have to deploy gateways or enable port monitoring.
- You must allow for the ATA memory and processing on your DC's, and that could involve adding resources to VM's or resizing cloud-based VM's.
- There is a sizing tool that works out how much traffic is taking place on your DC's.
- The lightweight gateway has silent installers and could be deployed to your DC's from a tool like SCCM/LANDesk.
- There are no rules, custom tuning, or any of the usual monitoring tool nonsense we usually have to deal with.
- The gateway option requires port mirroring, an extra VM and slightly more effort.
- The gateway/port mirroring option is harder to discover from a hacker's perspective.
- Installing the center and 10 lightweight gateways would take no more than a day.
- There is no dependency on Azure AD (AAD), you can deploy all of this to in-house AD only.

"It's the behavior pattern that ATA is looking for and while the type of attack changes constantly the phases remain the same".

It's possible for attackers to use common files types as an attack platform that behave in a suspicious fashion but would not be picked up by AV as a potential threat.

ATA feeds its alerts into the OMS Log space (OMS is covered in Chapter 12).

Type=SecurityDetection Type=SecurityDetection AlertSeverity=high AlertTitle="Suspicious Activity"

3 Results ☰ List ⠿ Table ▦ Security Detection

Detection Instance

ATA.bitc.local | 2/22/2017 7:48:37.740 AM   ⌄

Computer
ATA.bitc.local

Provider
Microsoft ATA

Time Generated
2/22/2017 7:48:37.740 AM

Alert Severity
High

Suspicious Activity
The following directory services enumerations using SAMR protocol were attempted against DC1 from DESKTOP-164P82E: Successful enumeration of all users in bitc.local by Administrator

2.4 The questions

- Do we have a security policy, or future desired end state for this tool?
- How does ATA fit into that policy or desired end state?
- Do we have any behavior profiling software in use right now?
- What is the end-to-end cost of the project going to be?
- What is the business case for this project and do we feel it's warranted?
- What do we need to run ATA in a POC?
- What is this going to cost from a licensing perspective?
- If we discover an intrusion now, what do we do?
- What third parties do we need to include/notify if we find an intrusion?
- If we discover an intrusion when the tool it is running and part of normal operations what is the procedure?
- What team is going to own this?
- How will it be reported on?
- Are we going to feed alerts from this into a different system?
- Will the team who monitor detections be the same as the team that remediates?
- Who will have visibility into the tool, its findings and the actions taken?

2.5 The mind map

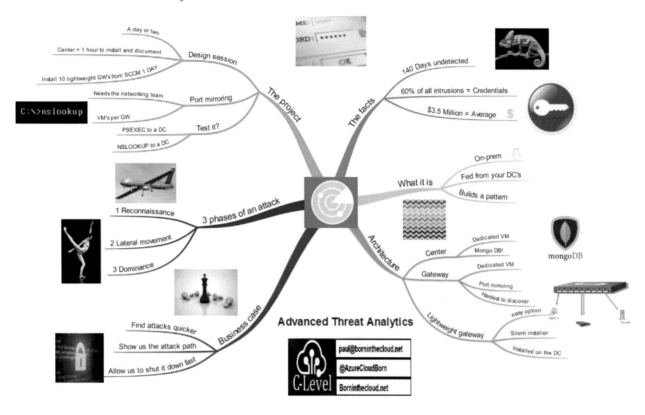

Advanced Threat Analytics

The project
- Design session
  - A day or two
  - Center = 1 hour to install and document
  - Install 10 lightweight GW's from SCCM 1 DAY
- Port mirroring
  - Needs the networking team
  - VM's per GW
- Test it?
  - PSEXEC to a DC
  - NSLOOKUP to a DC

`C:\>nslookup`

3 phases of an attack
- 1 Reconnaissance
- 2 Lateral movement
- 3 Dominance

Business case
- Find attacks quicker
- Show us the attack path
- Allow us to shut it down fast

The facts
- 140 Days undetected
- 60% of all intrusions = Credentials
- $3.5 Million = Average

What it is
- On-prem
- Fed from your DC's
- Builds a pattern

Architecture
- Center
  - Dedicated VM
  - Mongo DB!
- Gateway
  - Dedicated VM
  - Port mirroring
  - Hardest to discover
- Lightweight gateway
  - easy option
  - Silent installer
  - Installed on the DC

mongoDB

C-Level
- paul@borninthecloud.net
- @AzureCloudBorn
- Borninthecloud.net

Notes:

29

3.0 ADVANCED THREAT PROTECTION (ATP)

What is the problem that ATP is trying to solve?

If you are attacked, you need to answer three questions;

- How did it get here?
- What did it do?
- Where did it go?

ATP is going to show you who was attacked, what the attack was and where the attack has spread to.

Device	Windows Defender Advanced Threat Protection (to give it its full name) is a sensor on all Windows 10 anniversary devices; it connects to the ATP portal and shows you the health of your Windows 10 device. **This is a "Detection" tool.**

Service Name	Service Location	Endpoint Location
ATP	Cloud	On Premise

QR Code	Web location	Description
	https://www.youtube.com/watch?v=7QRVF3cO8xs	This is a short video on ATP at the Born In The Cloud YouTube channel

3.1 Introduction

Windows Defender Advanced Threat Protection (ATP) is built on the mindset of "Assume Breach". ATP is made up of 3 components;

1. A behavioral based sensor on Windows 10 Anniversary Edition (or higher)
2. Cloud security analytics portal in Azure (that you must connect your Win 10 devices to)
3. Microsoft and third party vendor's, security intelligence

3.2 In detail

ATP is a game changer in terms of leveling the playing field with the ever-evolving cybersecurity threats. ATP is a behavioral based sensor on all Windows 10 devices that looks for Advanced Persistent Threats (APT's). Each customer has its own ATP tenant in Azure that clients send data to. The sensor works alongside your Antivirus (AV) client to protect your endpoints. ATP works with the Microsoft AV agent, Windows Defender (yes, I know the naming is confusing☹) and any other third party AV provider. This point of working alongside your current AV is important to note, it does not replace your AV.

One of the key features of ATP is that it assumes breach, not only does it not shy away from the fact, the primary focus of the ATP portal is detecting a breach, showing its timeline, helping you investigate the spread and giving you the tools to respond. ATP's mindset is that attackers who have traditionally remained undetected in an organization for 100+ days will now be detected in near real time.

The "Active Alerts" screen allows us to very quickly identify an attack on our systems. In all the examples in our alerts page, we can see that there has obviously been a breach, with several events but they are still at the "phishing" stage so they are of a "Medium" security threat. If we then observed a pass - the - hash attack, for example it would go to High.

When investigating an incident, there are three questions that you must answer quickly;

1. How did it get here?
2. What did it do?
3. Where did it go?

You access ATP through https://securitycenter.windows.com, and once on the portal screen ATP Alerts and an incident graph will show you the files who's "behavior" has been identified as inappropriate. Attackers are using common files that are not identified as malware but are behaving in an inappropriate way.

ATP then has a cloud-based "Sandbox" called a detonation chamber. This isolated sandbox acts as a fully secure environment that will run the files and observe all the actions it takes thereafter. All of this is processed into an easy to read report.

ATP is also a forensic tool, as it will show you the attack and its timeline even if, as part of the attack, the program deletes itself.

You can buy ATP through a licensing SKU like Windows 10 E5 or Microsoft 365 Enterprise (please refer to your Microsoft account manager for this). Once you have signed up for the service you will receive onboarding instructions via email that will help you get your subscription ready for deployment.

The sensor that is installed and optimized on your Windows 10 device needs to be able to talk to your cloud service and to do that a small configuration file must be deployed to your devices.

Windows Defender ATP is a close relative of, but different to Office 365 ATP which is a similar service but for your Exchange Online environment and not for your Windows 10 endpoints. Office 365 ATP will block the spread of the attack using Exchange Online as the attack vector; this blocking capability is only being added to the Windows version as part of the latest Windows updated to Windows 10 (Creator update).

ATP was built on a "pivot wide" principle, meaning that from ATP you will be able to investigate an issue from ATP – Office ATP and back in-house to ATA (covered in chapter 2).

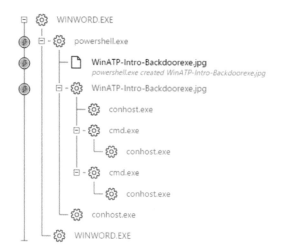

Inside the ATA console, we get to see the "Alert Process Tree". The process tree answers the question; how did it get here?

In this example, you can see the attack came in the form of a word doc with a macro that was enabled.

Creator Edition

The second major service update to Windows 10 called "Creator" was released in April 2017. With the new functionality of Windows Creator, ATP gets some amazing new functionality. Let's have a look at the new features.

- Detection – ATP gives us new memory and kernel sensors that allow us to detect attacks that just live in memory or those that sit in the kernel and are often in the dark from AV.
- Investigation – Windows Defender AV and Device Guard will now surface into the ATP console and help move us closer to the single pane of glass for security devices.
- Response – ATP now changes from a detection only tool to a response tool. We get the ability to isolate machines, block files, kill and quarantine processes that are under attack. We also get the ability to have an investigation package sent from the endpoint for forensic investigation.

Very cool work on behalf of the Windows 10 security team so please keep it up ☺.

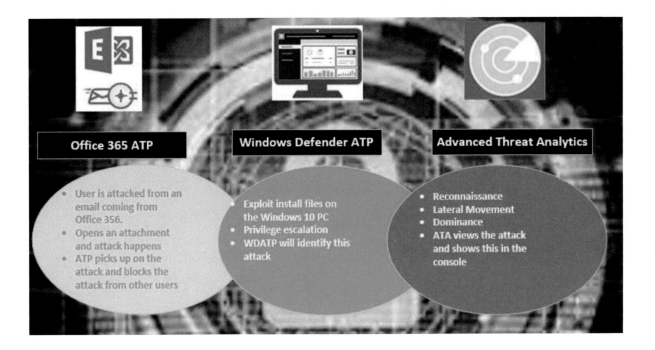

3.3 The project

ATP is a cloud-based service, and the sensor is part of the Windows 10. Assuming you already have Windows 10 deployed then the effort to enable ATP is easy. The project involves two steps;

1. Sign up for a tenant portal
2. Configure the sensor

Tenant Portal

The onboarding experience is fast and straightforward. It will deploy a new portal for your tenant, connect to your AAD and get you ready to start. When you sign up on the portal the onboarding process will ask you your industry sector, this is important as if it discovers a pattern of an entire industry being attacked it will alert you to this.

Configure the sensor

The sensor just needs to be configured to communicate to a specific Azure subscription. There are several ways to set this configuration;

1. Group Policy Object
2. System Center Configuration Manager (SCCM)
3. Windows Intune
4. A script that you download and run locally

Once the tenant is setup, there is a tab for Onboarding, on which can be found the configuration download package of choice. The package is less than 10Kb so deploying this to your estate is going to be simple. It's very likely that you can onboard 10,000 machines in a week from a single GPO setting with only a few hours of admin effort.

The incident graph shown here answers the question; where did it go? In this case, the attack spread to another three PC's.

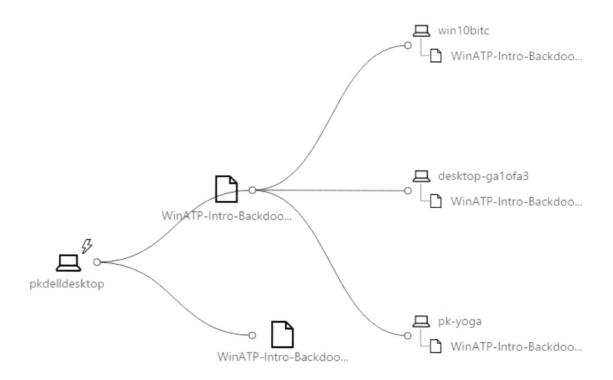

ATP, when used internally by Microsoft, was responsible for more than 50% of real security alerts on the client endpoint. We have never seen a tool that changes the game as much as ATP. Assume breach and ATP will help you find that breach.

3.4 The questions

- How widely deployed is Windows 10 Anniversary edition in our organization?
- What is the cost of deploying this service to our estate?
- What existing tools do we have that perform this breach diagnostics?
- How effective is our current toolset at breach investigation?
- How will we integrate with ATA and Office 365 ATP?
- What is the business case for this project?
- How will we verify what endpoints are missing or are not reporting in their state?
- Who will own this project?
- How are we going to deploy the configuration file?
- Who will monitor the portal?
- Will the same team monitor and act?
- How will we review breaches?
- Do our legal team understand the impact and can we engage them in a breach?
- Do we need to contact law enforcement if there is a breach?
- How will we interact with Microsoft's PSS in the event of a breach?

The "Machine View" allows you to quickly investigate the device at risk and what users have logged on to this endpoint. Once you know the users at risk, you can pivot to ATA to look further into their user accounts.

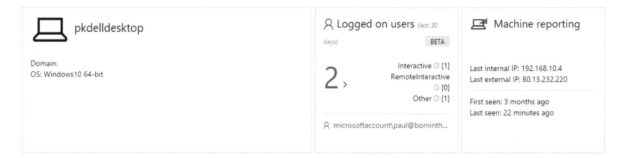

3.5 The mind map

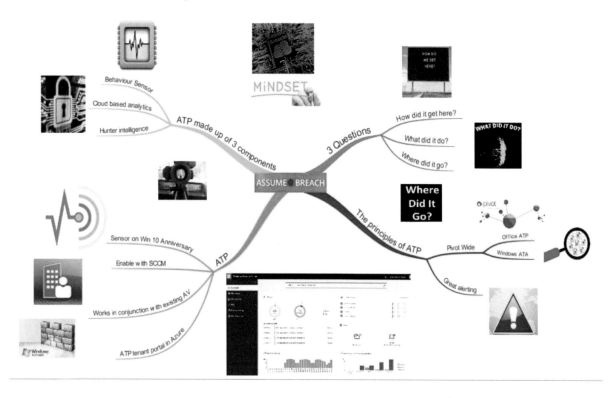

Behaviour Sensor
Cloud based analytics
Hunter intelligence

ATP made up of 3 components

MiNDSET

3 Questions

How did it get here?
What did it do?
Where did it go?

WHAT DID IT DO?

ASSUME • BREACH

Where
Did It
Go?

Sensor on Win 10 Anniversary
Enable with SCCM
Works in conjunction with existing AV

ATP

The principles of ATP

Office ATP

Pivot Wide

Windows ATA

Great alerting

ATP tenant portal in Azure

Notes:

4.0 O365 ADVANCED THREAT PROTECTION (O365 ATP)

What is the problem that O365 ATP is trying to solve?

O365 ATP is trying to stop email attacks arriving in from O365 in the form of attachments or links in the email.

Device	 User	O365 ATP will protect the device and the user who is using that device. It will protect the device from malware and the user's account from phishing. **This is a "Protection" tool.**

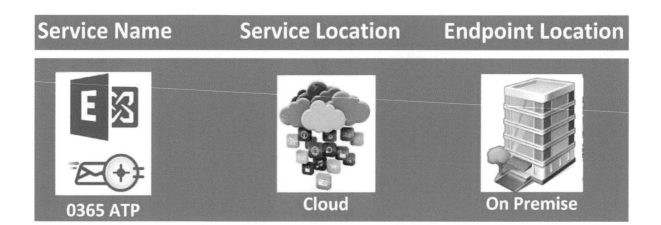

Service Name	Service Location	Endpoint Location
O365 ATP	Cloud	On Premise

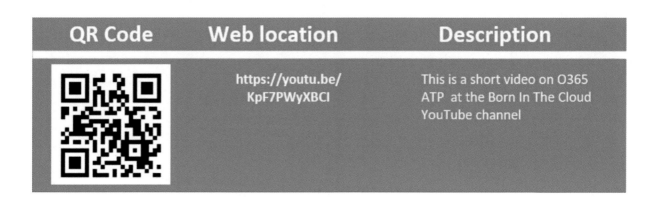

QR Code	Web location	Description
	https://youtu.be/ KpF7PWyXBCI	This is a short video on O365 ATP at the Born In The Cloud YouTube channel

4.1　Introduction

O365 ATP makes up the third side of the protection triangle that started by detecting an on-premises attack with ATA, it then covered an attack on the device with Windows Defender ATP and now we are stopping an attack vector through email with a very similar technology.

O365 ATP has a detonation chamber for attachments and can rewrite unsafe links preventing both attacks reaching the end user. While writing this book a ransomware attack called "WannaCry" crippled business worldwide, and it spread through email, and this email attack was stopped for ATP customers!

4.2　In detail

O365 ATP essentially comprises of a few web pages in the protection.office.com page, two tabs, "Safe Attachments" and "Safe Links" make up the sum of the configuration we need to consider.

At first glance, these two tabs look unassuming, but that is by design. The configuration and administration must be easy to understand but powerful in its implementation. Let's explore the process in a bit more detail.

Safe Attachments
Safe attachments begin with a policy that deals with what to do with attachments sent to a user via O365. The actions range from;

- Do nothing
- Monitor
- Block
- Replace
- Dynamic delivery

Once we decide what we are going to do with an attachment we can then decide who this applies to. A simple default policy could likely;

- Dynamically deliver the mail (with a notice that an attachment is being scanned and will be delivered shortly, if safe)
- Apply this at the enterprise level

This policy would inspect all attachments company-wide. A short delay would be experienced by all users of around 3-10 minutes for the attachment to be delivered but the email will arrive straightaway.

From the policy, we can monitor the results of the protection based on file type and what the attack was.

When I receive an email with an attachment, the mail gets delivered but the attachment needs to be scanned.

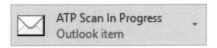

When used in conjunction with WD ATP, the O365 ATP suite offers an incredible security suite for the end user. This protection is extended to our mobile workforce with ease. The enormous scale of Office 365 means that Microsoft can feed the attack information into its security graph and use that knowledge to further build out its protection.

Safe Links
Phishing attacks in email are sent as an internet link that often looks legitimate but leads the end user to a nefarious location. Safe Links scans the URL and then cross references it with known attack locations.

Just like Safe Attachments, Safe Links is configured as a policy online. There are fewer options in Safe Links than Safe Attachments, and it's a very easy policy to configure. The policy settings allow us to;
- Use safe attachments
- Monitor the user clicks
- Prevent access to the link

Safe links verification happens in near real time and does not have the same delay as Safe Attachments does.

Default policy

general
▸ settings
applied to

Select the action for unknown potentially malicious URLs in messages.

○ Off

◉ On - URLs will be rewritten and checked against a list of
known malicious links when user clicks on the link.

☑ Use Safe Attachments to scan downloadable content.

☐ Do not track user clicks

☑ Do not allow users to click through to original URL

Do not rewrite the following URLs:

🖉 —

| Enter a valid URL | ✚ |

We get to monitor the URL navigation from emails through the O365 console.

Url Trace Results

🖉 ↻

TIME OF CLICK (UTC) ▼	RECIPIENT	URL	BLOCKED	CLICKED THROU...	MESSAGE ID
2/26/2017 10:43:04 AM	paul@borninthecloud.net	http://hackaday.com	No	No	<CAFBtqWZhR4
2/26/2017 10:42:55 AM	paul@borninthecloud.net	http://hackaday.com	No	No	<CAFBtqWZhR4l
2/26/2017 10:37:06 AM	paul@borninthecloud.net	https://elite-hackers.com/tools/	No	No	<CAFBtqWY+pH
2/26/2017 10:20:54 AM	paul@borninthecloud.net	http://WWW.BADGUY.COM	No	No	<CAFBtqWahG3l
2/26/2017 10:16:16 AM	paul@borninthecloud.net	http://www.fourhournewsletter.com/...	No	No	<s56ejelGvFQW!
2/26/2017 10:15:50 AM	paul@borninthecloud.net	http://www.fourhournewsletter.com/...	No	No	<s56ejelGvFQW!
2/26/2017 10:15:30 AM	paul@borninthecloud.net	http://www.fourhournewsletter.com/...	No	No	<s56ejelGvFQW!
2/26/2017 10:14:36 AM	paul@borninthecloud.net	http://www.fourhournewsletter.com/...	No	No	<s56ejelGvFQW!

4.3 The project

The project to deploy O365 is going to be easy. The settings options are not extensive and can be tested quite quickly.

We have implemented this project on an enterprise scale in a few weeks, ideally deploy this to your pre-prod O365 environment, test it and then look to roll this out to production. A timeframe of between 2-4 weeks would have the solution rolled out in pilot and give you enough of a data sample to understand the impact of deploying the different templates company-wide.

An email with an attachment and links, is sent to a user

The mail arrives in O365 and ATP takes over

The mail goes to a detonation chamber, and once verified gets sent to the user

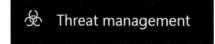

The links get verified and possibly rewritten and then sent on to the end user

4.4 The questions

- How do we scan attachments and links today?
- How can we implement O365 ATP to a pilot group?
- How will we deal with attachments that have been stopped?
- Will we communicate with the sender that this has been blocked?
- What do we need to communicate with the helpdesk about this?
- What do we do if an attachment has been blocked but we still want it?
- What additional licensing do we need to add to use this technology?
- Who will deploy this?
- How will we monitor the blocks?
- How will we report to the business on its effectiveness?
- How will our end users respond to a delay in documents via email?

4.5 The mind map

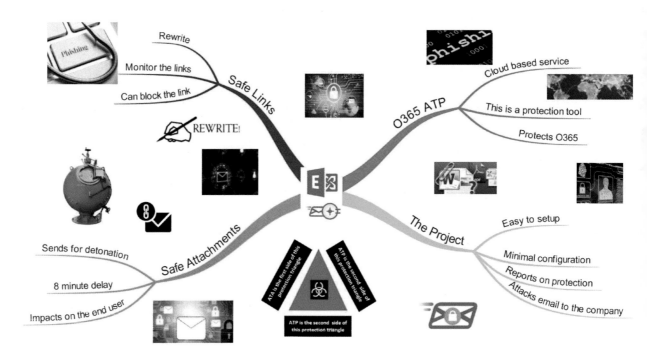

Notes:

5.0 AZURE ACTIVE DIRECTORY (AAD)

What is the problem that AAD is trying to solve?

AAD is seeking to solve several issues all stemming from an outdated directory model that is Active Directory. The problems that AAD solves are;

- Single Sign On (SSO) to both cloud and on-premises applications
- Easily share resources with partners and customers
- Self-service for a few user functions like password reset and group management

 Azure Active Directory focuses on the user. AAD can protect both cloud only and on premise users. AAD is used as the single identity for applications, can be used with Multi Factor Authentication (MFA) and can report on suspicious user activity. **This is a "Protection" tool**

User

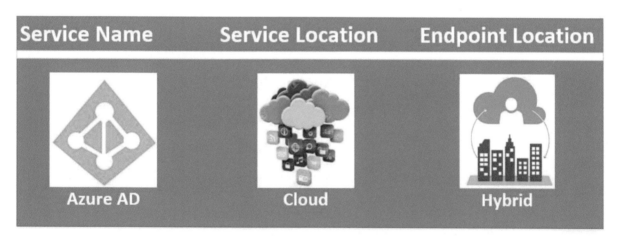

Service Name	Service Location	Endpoint Location
Azure AD	Cloud	Hybrid

QR Code	Web location	Description
	https://www.youtube.com/watch?v=21FqHJzQ11w&feature=youtu.be	This is a short video on Azure AD at the Born In The Cloud YouTube channel

5.1 Introduction

AAD is a cloud version of Active Directory (AD). You can install AAD in an azure subscription and have no integration with an on- premises AD or you can connect your on-premises AD to AAD.

- This is a multi-tenant directory.
- AD can replicate users and groups via AD Connect to AAD.
- It offers application federation and publishing.
- It offers SSO to a multitude of cloud-based Software as a Service (SaaS) app's like Salesforce and ServiceNow.
- It offers a range of self-service options around areas like password reset & group management.
- Authentication can remain in-house with Active Directory Federation Services (ADFS).
- It is regularly referred to as an identity bridge as it can act as the connector to many different services.

As Azure AD migrates to the new portal we get the more familiar color schemes and updated views.

Users and groups

5.2 In detail

So far, we have spoken about security solutions like ATP and ATA where the user data is not going to the cloud. With O365 and with AAD, we are talking about replicating you're on-premises AD to the cloud, so your users and groups are going to be replicated to AAD. Why? Because by using AAD we can take advantage of several key security areas that only Microsoft can offer.

- The Microsoft security graph

In the earlier section of this book that covered the Microsoft Security Graph, we learned how Microsoft are collecting telemetry data from around the globe at a scale that makes them unique in terms of the size of their authentication engine. They are using "big data" to manage the size and scale of the data points in an efficient manner and then using machine learning to write and re-write security rules at speeds previously consider the imagination of sci-fi movies.

We can publish both SaaS and on-prem web applications via AAD.

Applications published through AAD, get summarized on the Enterprise applications page.

Publishing the web applications that exist inside your data center means that users can access those apps externally, but with all the protection of the Security Graph

Microsoft uses this immense security knowledge to protect user identities in AAD, and you can avail of this service right now. Many of the security tools in the coming chapters are predicated on an existing AAD being in place and as such, if you don't already have AAD then this needs to go on your roadmap pretty darn soon! Right now, on-premises AD is still king in terms of functionality like GPO, OU's etc. However, this is going to change, and in the future AAD will become the central directory structure and the on-premises versions will be far less feature rich (this is the author's opinion and that of many MVP's but should not be taken as an official roadmap statement on AAD).

Most organizations that have already deployed AAD have done so as a prerequisite to an Office365 deployment, in this basic mode you get several security features; however, a lot of the advanced security features in the book require advanced security SKU's in the Office365 suite.

Active Directory started out life in Windows 2000 when the world was a different place. The remote worker was a dream and work centered around the corporate office. Today we are using more cloud-based resources from ServiceNow to Workday, to Dropbox to Office 365. In a world where authentication only happened on-premises this cloud and mobile world would find it very hard to verify a user's identity, and then keep it secure.

You do not need to be migrating to Exchange Online to use AAD, it can be deployed and used for;

- SSO to cloud apps
- Publishing internal web apps
- MFA to cloud and on-premises resources
- Conditional access to cloud-based SaaS apps
- Mobile Device Management (covered in detail in Chapter 9)
- Self Service password reset with write-back capabilities to on-premises AD
- Self-Service group management
- Advanced security reporting
- AAD domain join for Windows 10 devices
- Provisioning partner authentication access
- Provisioning client based identifies

5.3 The project

AAD starts off with a tenant in Azure that you will either already have or your Microsoft team will happily get ready for you. You may already be using Azure compute and not have AAD so if you already have several subscriptions you need to plan a little what subscription you are going to place AAD in.

The project starts with deploying AD Connect. This essentially replicates you're on-premises AD to AAD. One of the main questions that people need to answer is who do you want to control authenticating user from AAD. There are two options;

1. Let AAD perform the authentication, this is the simplest, default option. It's very simple, you pass the responsibility to Microsoft and that's all there is to it. This is the only option you have if you are using Microsoft O365 Business.
2. The second option is to deploy ADFS, this essentially tells AAD when a user tires to authenticate via AAD, to send the authentication back to ADFS servers that are member servers of an on-premises AD. In this option, you get more control of the authentication process, however, you are now responsible for the ADFS servers and in turn the authentication process. The ADFS model is certainly the flavor of the month in most organizations and the ADFS environment is generally used or at least available for federated authentication purposes in the future. It is also now very common to build out the ADFS environment in Azure as an IaaS solution and take advantage of the high availability of the cloud.

The backend process of setting up the replication and authentication models is not that big a deal, however, there may be a large on-boarding process, and end user training for tools like the myapps.microsoft.com page. This is the self-service landing page for end users to perform actions like;

1. Self-service password reset and recovery setup tasks
2. SSO access to published applications
3. Group management

Let's look at a couple of simple and common use cases for AAD.

"Our company has several SaaS apps and that number is growing, how can I provision SSO and maybe ask for greater security for some apps while not requiring it for others?"

With AAD you can configure federations to thousands of 3rd party apps many of which are Microsoft competitors like Google, AWS, and Salesforce. With AAD you can specify MFA etc. for certain apps. With social media apps like Twitter or Facebook, it's possible to allow AAD to manage the passwords for you with a feature called "password rollover". With this model, you publish access to the Twitter app through the "myapps" portal, if the user leaves the company you remove access to the AAD account and then all the SaaS apps are gone.

"We have critical internal web applications and we need to increase security to them, some of them are pretty standard but some are a bit bespoke, Azure AD looks great for SaaS but am I looking for something else for my on-premises web apps?"

AAD can be used to federate SaaS apps but equally, we can also publish on-premises applications and publish custom apps your company develops. If your web app has issues publishing Microsoft have created a partnership with Ping Identities whereby you can use the Ping toolset to publish your on-premises apps.

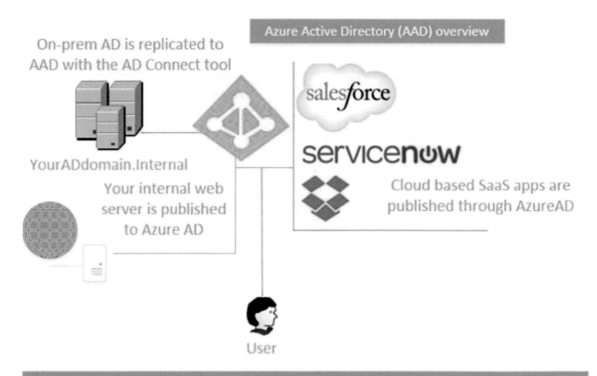

When the user goes to myapps.microsoft.com, they can access internal apps, thousands of web based SaaS apps and self service activities like password change or recovery and group management.

5.4 The questions

- What is the business case for deploying AAD?
- What are the risks to our company by replicating our internal directory to Azure?
- What are the features of AAD we are going to deploy?
- Are we going to manage the authentication or let AAD do it, and why?
- If we deploy ADFS how much high availability do we need?
- What other advanced Azure security tools do we want to use that require AAD?
- Who will own the AAD project, and when it's up and running who will own the service?
- How will we monitor the ADConnect replication process?
- How will we manage password write back?
- What problems in our company will AAD resolve?
- How critical to our business is the AAD project?
- If we don't deploy AAD what are the security implications to the business?
- Do we have an existing password self-service and recovery tool?

AAD seems like a pretty simple concept; replicate your users to the cloud, big deal. However, to just view Azure AD as a basic cloud-based user repository for access to Office 365 is a not doing AAD justice. When AAD is being used as an identity bridge, and this identity bridge is powered by the Microsoft Intelligent Security Graph, we get an authentication model we could only dream off before the cloud.

5.5 The mind map

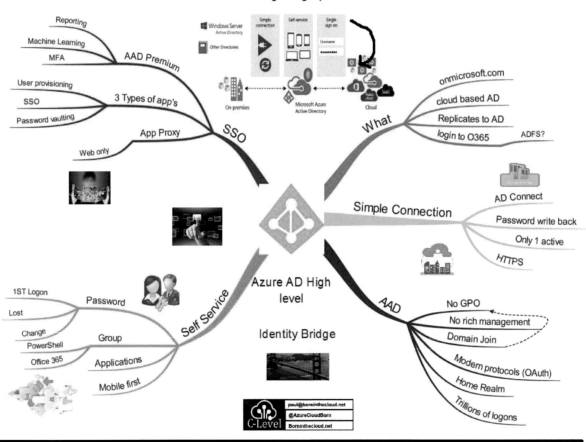

Notes:

6.0 AAD IDENTITY PROTECTION (AAD-IP)

What is the problem that AAD Identity Protection (AAD-IP) is trying to solve?

AAD-IP is trying to keep users safe with as little additional security checks as possible (visible to the user). It monitors the user login and if it sees any unusual behavior it applies additional security to that user, or in some cases even blocks the login and asks the users to provide MFA or in some cases contact the help desk.

User	Azure Active Directory Identity Protection focuses on the user. AAD-IP can protect both cloud only and on premise users. AAD-IP is dependent on Azure AD, and places an additional layer of behaviour modelling into the authentication process. **This is a "Protection" tool.**

Service Name	Service Location	Endpoint Location
Identity Protection	Cloud	Cloud

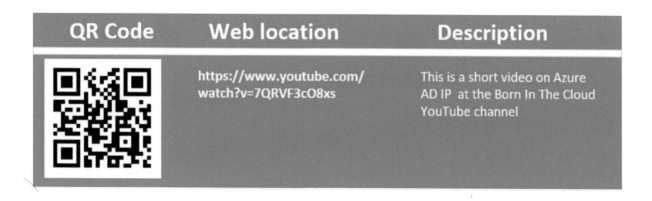

QR Code	Web location	Description
	https://www.youtube.com/watch?v=7QRVF3cO8xs	This is a short video on Azure AD IP at the Born In The Cloud YouTube channel

6.1 Introduction

The majority of security breaches take place when an attacker gets access to a valid username and password. AAD-IP takes advantage of the security graph by interrogating the login process to determine;

- Is the user account at risk/for sale in public?
- Are the conditions of the login risky?

6.2 In detail

AAD-IP is one of, if not our most favorite tool in the suite, because you don't know it's there until you need it. Enabling MFA for every user and enforcing for every login grows old, quickly. Sure, I want security, but only when I need it.

Vulnerabilities ⓘ

3

RISK LEVEL	COUNT	VULNERABILITY
Medium	15	Users without multi-factor authentication registration
Low	8	Administrators aren't using their privileged roles
Low	6	There are too many global administrators

On the "Overview" page we start with the vulnerabilities. This is a great starting point for assessing the health of our user estate.

When Brad Anderson (Corporate VP at Microsoft) spoke at Ignite 2016, the analogy he used was the safety features in a car. You want them to work when you need them, but not impede the normal driving experience. That is exactly what AAD-IP does, it lets you login and access your data with as little fuss as possible, but when it notices something amiss it will either challenge you for MFA or as for a password reset or if the threat is big enough block your access and ask you to contact your IT department.

I had MFA configured on my Azure tenant and as soon as I started to work with AAD-IP I now get challenged for MFA once in every 100 logins or less. It just feels liberating not to have to get the code from my phone all the time.

In mid-2016 Yahoo got hacked with over one billion user accounts and passwords placed on the web, two of which were mine☹. As part of that attack they also got everyone's password reset questions too. This is problematic because I can't change things like where I went to school, my first car, movie etc. The reason they were good questions is that the answers were real. Now those answers are on the dark web somewhere, frightening!

What if you had user accounts that were part of the exposé? What if your users have the same password in-house with AD? Microsoft build databases of these accounts that are often for sale on the internet and bring this data into AAD-IP. If you know that your user's identity is for sale you can look to change passwords, and enforce stricter controls over that user and use tools like ATA and ATP to investigate the user's in-house activities.

With AAD-IP we get fantastic visualizations that show the impact of policies and how many users have been challenged to date.

Visualize the impact of the current policy configuration

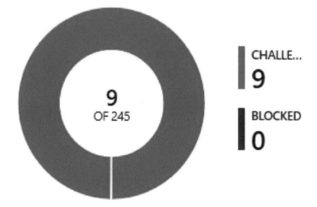

9
OF 245

CHALLE...
9

BLOCKED
0

If on the other hand, there is no indication of the user account being at risk, maybe the login itself seems risky. If I login from London every day and a few minutes later I am trying the same login from Russia this needs investigation. If I am trying to login with an anonymous IP address this needs to be looked at too. If either of these situations are true, then I will be challenged for MFA. If the MFA challenge results in a successful login, then AAD will learn about the new location and stop further challenges.

With AAD-IP you set policies for certain risk level, and then configure what protective action should be applied when that risk level is reached. The policy is then applied to users and thereby you start protecting your users. Once again, we see the Microsoft Security Graph in action. Billions of logins being stored in big data, mind blowing analytics and machine learning changing the rules on the fly. Welcome to the new world!

This product can be bought and applied to specific users, so maybe you might start with just the high value accounts in your company. As it's easy to get working why not pilot it on the C-Level in your company first

With AAD-IP there are essentially 3 questions that will be asked;

1. What is the risk level?
2. What will we do?
3. Who is affected?

Here is an example of the unfamiliar locations outputs from the tool.

	USER	IP	LOCATION	SIGN-IN TIME (UTC)
	Paul Keely	37.228.226.24	Dublin, County Dublin, Irela...	12/25/2016 7:55 AM
	Paul Keely	5.133.242.9	Great Dunmow, England, Un...	12/15/2016 11:01 AM
	Paul Keely	191.96.249.110	Victoria, Seychelles	12/7/2016 8:59 PM
	Paul Keely	50.235.236.67	FL, United States	12/7/2016 5:50 PM
	Paul Keely	146.185.163.44	Amsterdam, North Holland, ...	11/7/2016 6:23 PM
	Paul Keely	167.220.152.42	Redmond, WA, United States	▶ 3 instances

We start off by asking what is the risk level and what activity is associated with this risk? You can then decide on a policy that matches this risk. Two simple examples of this are;

- Authentication requests from unfamiliar locations
- Authentication requests from anonymous locations

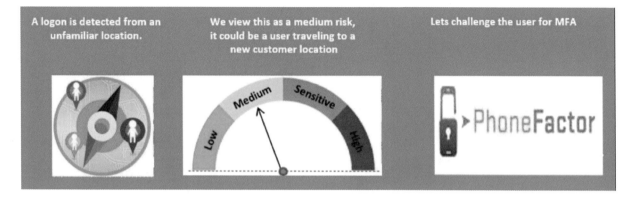

6.3 The project

AAD is the pre-requisite of AAD-IP so if that is already in place then the hard work has already been done. To get this "Identity Protection" protecting your users you need a specific license (best ask your MS account team). This product is easy to setup, easy to understand and easy to implement.

In terms of a time frame estimate, the design sessions, design and pilot is less than a week. It could most likely be rolled out to 10,000 users over a few weeks. You need to make sure that there is an end user education process that includes an awareness that you may be challenged for MFA, that you may be asked to change your password and that we may even block your access.

There is no doubt that the registration for MFA and end user education is going to be a pretty big part of this project and this "soft skills" side of the project will over shadow? the technical requirements. The risk events show in the image below the number of authentications from unknown and anonymous locations. If a user travels to a new location, they will be challenged for an MFA and once that is logged they will not be challenged again.

RISK LEVEL	DETECTION TYPE	RISK EVENT TYPE	RISK EVENTS CLOSED	LAST UPDATED (UTC)
Medium	Real-time	Sign-ins from anonymous IP addresses ❶	10 of 10	25/02/2017, 7:55 am
Medium	Real-time	Sign-ins from unfamiliar locations ❶	7 of 7	25/02/2017, 7:54 am

6.4 The questions

- Do we have any way of identifying or cross referencing if any of our user's accounts are currently for sale on the internet?
- Do we have any way of identifying or cross referencing if any of our user's personal accounts are currently for sale?
- Do you have a way of identifying potential hot spots or known rouge IP addresses that our users are trying to VPN from?
- Do we have any current way of responding with additional challenges to suspect logins?
- Do we have any mechanism (manual or automated) of disabling an account if we fear it has been compromised?
- If we enforce a policy to block end users, how will we communicate this to our end users?
- If/when end users get blocked how will they contact IT?
- When they do make contact how do we verify their identity?
- How will we communicate with high-level accounts that this policy is in place?
- Have we MFA set up and registered for the potentially affected users?

Review the current registration status

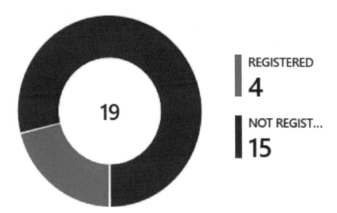

Before you enforce MFA, you can verify how many users have registered for the service in the first place. This is going to reduce helpdesk calls. In this case we have 15 users not registered and so enabling this policy now will result in a poor user experience.

Freeing up users from being required to use MFA for every login, and instead only being prompted when there is a possible threat shows how the security graph works. This is security that you can't see. It is just like a curtain of airbags in a car, it only engages when needed. More tools like this please Microsoft!

Each week AAD-IP will mail you a digest of the week's activities. We find it a great overview every weekend of what is going on with our user's identities.

6.5 The mind map

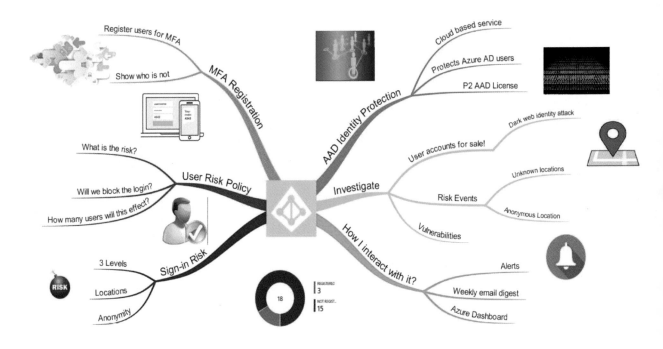

Register users for MFA
Show who is not
MFA Registration

Cloud based service
Protects Azure AD users
P2 AAD License
AAD Identity Protection

What is the risk?
Will we block the login?
How many users will this effect?
User Risk Policy

User accounts for sale!
Dark web identity attack
Unknown locations
Risk Events
Anonymous Location
Vulnerabilities
Investigate

3 Levels
Locations
Anonymity
Sign-in Risk

Alerts
Weekly email digest
Azure Dashboard
How I interact with it?

REGISTERED
3
NOT REGIST.
15
18

Notes:

7.0 AAD PRIVILEGED IDENTITY MANAGEMENT (AAD-PIM)

What is the problem that AAD Privileged Identity Management (PIM) is trying to solve?

In traditional IT, we add users to groups and leave them there. PIM will give a user access to a group but only for a certain period, and only to the group they need. This is often referred to as;

- "Just in Time" (JIT) administration
- Least privilege

USER

Azure AD Privileged Identity Management is looking to reduce the payoff from attacking a privileged account. This is going to help protect the user. **This is a "Protection" tool.**

Service Name	Service Location	Endpoint Location
Privileged Identity	Cloud	Cloud

QR Code	Web location	Description
	https://www.youtube.com/watch?v=R5FzDkOJFkE&list=PL2VFYXnuRMkLgq8GlZFhRtUBwKyvy3htP&index=7	This is a short video on Azure PIM at the Born In The Cloud YouTube channel

7.1 Introduction

It is not uncommon to find large numbers of user accounts in groups like Domain Admins or other "supper user" type accounts. What is also not surprising is to find users that left the organization still being members of security groups that afford them the capabilities to do nearly everything. In Server 2016's version of Active Directory we can time restrict group access and we can similarly also do the same in AAD with PIM.

At Ignite 2016 Microsoft claimed that they had no full-time admins on any server, and we were impressed. "Just in Time" administration both in-house and in the cloud, had come of age.

It's time to remove full time admins in your organization.

AAD PIM has the simplest overview page with just three main task options that allow you to activate roles for "Just in Time" administration.

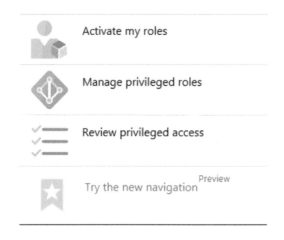

7.2 In detail

Domain admins, SQL DBA's and network administrators are the ultimate prize for hackers. Being a member of any of these groups will increase your vulnerability to hacking. It must be every organization's goal to have zero permanent admins.

How can we accomplish this?

Your admins are identified as "eligible" for a role not "permanently" in the role. When an admin wants access to a role they;

- Apply for the elevation for a period of, for example, 2 hours
- We ask them to use MFA
- We ask them for a ticket ID
- We ask them for justification for access (what work will be done)

After the allowed period, they are removed from the role and if they need to continue working in the role they reactivate. If their account was compromised (and we always assume breach) the attacker gets blocked as soon as the allotted period is over.

AAD PIM has the potential to become a lot deeper in terms of its enterprise adoption as it can be accessed programmatically, meaning that you could request and be granted a privilege from something like PowerShell. What this means to you is that you could have a process where I submit a service request to change an environment in an automated fashion and as part of the change process, the service account being used to perform the automation could be granted access to make changes and be automatically given privileges just for the requested time interval.

Roles

CLICK TO VIEW ALL ROLES

7 of 28

ROLE NAME	MFA ENABLED	USERS	ACTIVE	ELIGIBLE
Security Administrator	Yes	1	1 (100%)	0 (0%)
Global Administrator	Yes	6	1 (17%)	5 (83%)
Skype for Business Admini...	Yes	1	0 (0%)	1 (100%)
Device Administrators	Yes	1	1 (100%)	0 (0%)
Privileged Role Administra...	Yes	1	1 (100%)	0 (0%)
Service Administrator	Yes	1	0 (0%)	1 (100%)
SharePoint Service Admini...	Yes	1	0 (0%)	1 (100%)

Having permanent group access to the "Global Administrators" group for O365 is a dangerous line to walk. This group has power over your O365 environment that needs to be taken very seriously.

Let's have a look at the process and what we need to do.

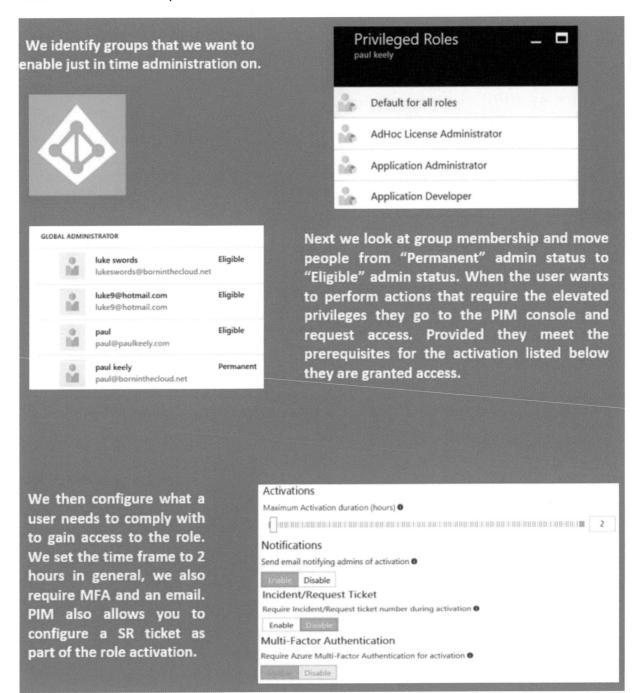

We identify groups that we want to enable just in time administration on.

Privileged Roles
paul keely

- Default for all roles
- AdHoc License Administrator
- Application Administrator
- Application Developer

GLOBAL ADMINISTRATOR

luke swords lukeswords@borninthecloud.net	Eligible
luke9@hotmail.com luke9@hotmail.com	Eligible
paul paul@paulkeely.com	Eligible
paui keely paul@borninthecloud.net	Permanent

Next we look at group membership and move people from "Permanent" admin status to "Eligible" admin status. When the user wants to perform actions that require the elevated privileges they go to the PIM console and request access. Provided they meet the prerequisites for the activation listed below they are granted access.

We then configure what a user needs to comply with to gain access to the role. We set the time frame to 2 hours in general, we also require MFA and an email. PIM also allows you to configure a SR ticket as part of the role activation.

Activations
Maximum Activation duration (hours) ●

2

Notifications
Send email notifying admins of activation ●
[Enable] Disable

Incident/Request Ticket
Require Incident/Request ticket number during activation ●
[Enable] Disable

Multi-Factor Authentication
Require Azure Multi-Factor Authentication for activation ●
[Enable] Disable

We have found that IT admins feel like there is a trust issue when we look to remove their "full time" group membership. Whilst this is understandable, if admins are made fully aware of the protection being offered to them by AAD-PIM from the start, it will dramatically reduce any ill-feeling. Information has a neutralizing effect.

The "Reviews" below show us when someone asked for access to a group for a specific period.

HEALTH CHECK				
Global Administrator	paul keely paul@borninthecloud.net	13/10/2016	12/11/2016	Complete
INTUNE ADMINS FOR LUKE				
Intune Service Administrator	paul keely paul@borninthecloud.net	24/01/2017	24/02/2017	Complete
SECURITY ADMINS				
Security Administrator	paul keely paul@borninthecloud.net	13/10/2016	12/11/2016	Complete

7.3 The project

In our experience, AAD-PIM needs a little more time to work out and explore than AAD-IP, especially when deployed in conjunction with the on prem version of 'just in time' admin with Server 2016 Active Directory.

AAD-PIM comes with and Azure P2 license and, just like AAD-IP it comes with a 'getting started' wizard. It's a blade or feature in the Azure portal that you enable. Once it's in place it's reasonably easy to work out how to use it. However, in contrast to AAD-IP where ideally nobody should notice that it's in place, admins will notice the AAD-PIM is in place because certain actions will require them to   go through the PIM process.

For cloud services like O365 we have found that the roles it protects are of such high value and the number of users that should be in those roles is so few that the impact should be small.

This project is going to apply to IT admins that understand technology. It is not for the entire end user estate like AAD-IP, so there is less of a communication plan needed.

The design, implementation and testing should take between one to four weeks (roughly a week to design and implement and then a few weeks of tweaking, adjustment and user knowledge transfer).

If you wanted to go beyond the basic web interface and move into programmatically interacting with AAD-PIM that is a far more complex and time consuming process and is beyond the scope of this book but get in contact and we will be happy to help.

GLOBAL ADMINISTRATOR

luke swords lukeswords@borninthecloud.net	Eligible	
luke9@hotmail.com luke9@hotmail.com	Eligible	
paul paul@paulkeely.com	Eligible	
paul keely paul@borninthecloud.net	Permanent	
rkuehfus@live.com rkuehfus@live.com	Eligible	
rob rob@borninthecloud.net	Eligible	

7.4 The questions

- What process will we have to change or implement to enable "Just in Time" administration?
- Have we MFA setup and registered for the potentially affected users?
- Will we require a ticket and if so what type of request is this potentially going to be (incident request, service request etc.)?
- Are we going to do this in conjunction with an enterprise-wide PIM or 'Just in Time' project, spanning Active Directory as well as the cloud?
- How will we review and monitor the AAD-PIM environment?
- Will many users remain as "Permanent" in the system?
- How will we communicate the change to our admin teams?
- What is the likely effort for our organization to implement this?
- In terms of risk assessment, how much risk do we feel we are in if we do not implement this?

As admin accounts are the number 1 target for attackers, reducing the prize of an admin account is a pretty high priority. To reduce the impact of an attack on an admin account we need to limit its group membership.

7.5 The mind map

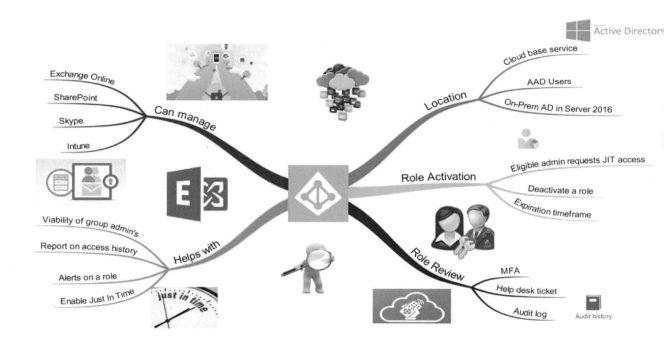

Notes:

8.0 MICROSOFT CLOUD APP SECURITY (CAS)

What is the problem that the Microsoft Cloud App Security is trying to solve?

With business focus moving towards a cloud and mobility, it is becoming increasingly difficult for IT to control and manage applications being used by employees and how the data is shared. Microsoft Cloud App Security provides enterprise-grade visibility, control and protection for your company's data in the cloud and mobility environments. It provides insight into what your cloud environment comprises. It shows what sanctioned or non-sanctioned applications your employees are using and provides risk assessment for these applications. It also provides access control to automate the protection of the data and access.

Protect Document	The CASB is focused on your data. **This is a "Protection", "Detection" and "Response" tool.**

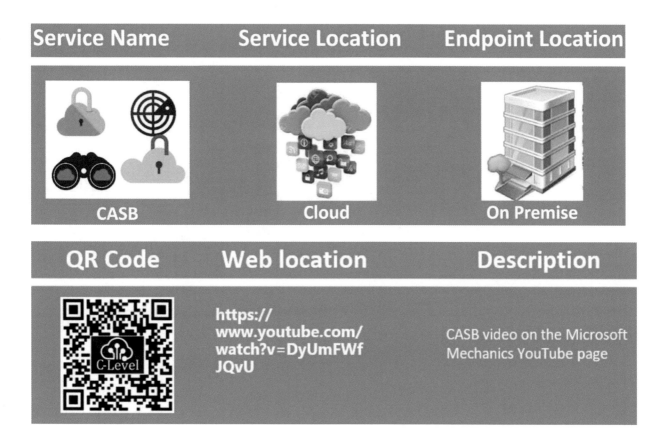

Service Name	Service Location	Endpoint Location
CASB	Cloud	On Premise

QR Code	Web location	Description
	https:// www.youtube.com/ watch?v=DyUmFWf JQvU	CASB video on the Microsoft Mechanics YouTube page

8.1 Introduction

Cloud App Security is Microsoft's CASB (Cloud App Security Broker) solution that provides a complete framework to secure your cloud applications. It acts as a gatekeeper, allowing the organization to extend the reach of it's security policies beyond it's own infrastructure. The solution provides 4 key functions:

1. **Cloud Discovery** – Discovers all cloud usage in your organization.
   It helps answers the question, what is my cloud environment? It provides information about how many cloud applications, sanctioned or non-sanctioned, are being used in the environment and what users are using these applications. It discovers the "Shadow IT" within your organization. For example,. if your organization sanctioned OneDrive, then how many users are still using Dropbox.

2. **Information Protection** – Monitor and Control your data in the Cloud.
   It gives you tools to protect the data. It shows how to ensure protection even with the use of sanctioned cloud applications. You can view the data breaches in your environment and immediately remediate them. For example, an employee trying to share a confidential document using a public link in Dropbox.

3. **Control** – Control and limit user access based on session context.
   It provides granular access control based on the data being accessed and the trust level of the request. For example, an employee trying to download a document from an untrusted public machine.

4. **Threat Detection** – Detect usage anomalies and security incidents.
   It identifies threats that are found in cloud environments and alerts the system administrators for remediation. For example, if there is an unusual number of requests from a bot to access your environment.

Right now, in your environment, it's very likely that users have subscribed to cloud services, and have company information on those services. Who is accessing that data? Where is it? How do we control access to it? Probably the most important question of all, is if the employee leaves how do we reclaim our data?

8.2 In detail

Business trends see traditional IT is shifting from in-house to cloud, and even if an organization doesn't use cloud-based solutions the employees still use one or more cloud-based SaaS applications (i.e. Software as a Service). These apps are becoming essential to today's connected business world. But these applications also introduce a unique set of security concerns. The legacy security solutions simply aren't designed to manage these concerns.

Like managing an on-premises enterprise environment where you need to maintain visibility, control, and protection, the same applies to the cloud. Microsoft Cloud App Security takes these concepts and extends them to your cloud applications. It provides you with:

1. Cloud App Discovery - to discover all the cloud apps being used in your network. You gain visibility into Shadow IT and assess risks.
2. Information Protection – to protect your data.
3. Data Control - to shape your cloud environment.
4. Threat Protection - to identify high-risk usage and cloud security issues.

Cloud App Discovery

Cloud App security identifies the cloud applications being used by the employees in your organization. It discovers cloud apps in use across your networks. It investigates user and sources IP cloud usage. It also provides risk assessment for more than 13,000 cloud applications. It discovers and provides risk assessment without the need to install any agents anywhere. All the information is collected from the firewalls and proxies, so it integrates with your network appliances. You can either manually upload the traffic logs to analyze them or you can configure to collect these logs from your appliance automatically.

It can also gather information directly from your application using APIs via it's App Connectors. These allow connecting to the Cloud applications without affecting the traffic between your users and the application. You can get full visibility into your cloud applications, no matter where these are being accessed e.g. managed and approved devices, remotely from mobile devices, unmanaged devices, within browsers or mobile applications.

Data is collected in one or all of the following ways:

- Manual Traffic Log Uploads - If there are requirements to analyze older traffic logs from network appliances then those are uploaded manually and reports are generated for these.
- Automatic Traffic Log Uploads - Automatic log uploads are configured from within the CASB portal so that the reports are generated based on the most up-to-date transactions. For this option, a virtual machine (either for VMWare or Hyper-V) is setup on-premises using the configuration from the Microsoft Cloud App Security portal. This VM is called the Log Collector. This machine sends all the data to the dataset in the Cloud App Security portal for analysis.
- Directly from App Connectors - As discussed, you can also connect a sanctioned app via App Connector in Cloud App Security. Various options include Office 365, Box, Microsoft OneDrive for Business, Microsoft Exchange Online, Microsoft Skype for Business, Amazon Web Services, Dropbox, Google Apps, Okta, Salesforce, ServiceNow, etc. Files, Activity and Accounts information is collected via APIs and analyzed.

You can discover all SaaS applications used in your environment and get a risk assessment. This automated risk assessment is done via a Risk Score by evaluating each discovered service against more than sixty parameters.

You also get powerful ongoing reporting analytics capabilities. These provide you with the complete context of your cloud usage. These reports include various criteria such as usage patterns, download/upload traffic and top uploading/downloading users etc. It gives you anomalous usage alerts. It also shows new apps as well as trending apps in your environments.

When a department wants an application, and can get it immediately, versus a typical IT project that lasts weeks/months/years why would they chose an IT driven internal service. I have worked with several IT departments that now have the goal of being "the best IT provider to the business", as opposed to "the only" IT provider to the business.

Control and Information Protection

Once you see exactly how your company is operating in the cloud, you can maintain control by determining which apps to sanction. Then you can set granular policies to control and protect your data. You can either use out of the box policies or build and customize your own.

There are 5 different types of policies that you can apply:
- Activity
- Anomaly detection
- App discovery
- Cloud discovery anomaly detection
- File

Any policy violations can create alerts whenever they occur and you can take actions to mitigate the risk on a file level. You can also investigate any related activities.

E.g. If a sensitive information is shared via a file on a public cloud platform (like OneDrive or Dropbox), then that can automatically be trapped via Cloud App Security and then you can either quarantine the file or make it private. You can also remove permissions from the collaborators of the sensitive file or even remove the file altogether.

For information protection, Microsoft Cloud App Security integrates with Azure Information Protection, Office 365 Information Protection and any third-party Data Loss Prevention and Protection software (DLPs).

Threat Detection

Cloud App Security also provides Threat Protection for your cloud apps, enhanced by Microsoft's vast amount of security intelligence and research from the Graph. You can identify high-risk usage, anomalies, detect abnormal user behavior and ward off threats. Cloud App Security's advanced machine learning algorithms learn how each user interacts with each of the SaaS applications. Then through a behavior analysis, it assesses the risk in each transaction.

E.g. A privileged user trying to access the private network from an anonymous location and trying to unsuccessfully login multiple times from different geographic locations within an hour will be trapped as a high-level threat.

It integrates with Microsoft Intelligent Security Graph and any third-party security information and event management systems (SIEMs).

Microsoft Cloud App Security provides comprehensive enterprise-grade security for Microsoft applications like Office 365 as well as third party cloud apps. It provides advanced security management capabilities for Office 365 apps via its deep integration. Cloud App Security is a great addition to Microsoft's mobility and security solution set. This solution set contains other solutions like Azure Rights Management, Azure Active Directory and Advanced Threat Analytics. These solutions work together to deliver a holistic and agile security platform. Cloud App Security is also available as a separate standalone subscription.

8.3 The project

A typical project will involve discussing the licensing requirements. Microsoft Cloud App Security is available as a part of EMS E5 (Enterprise Mobility and Security) or as a standalone product. If the organization already owns an EMS E5 license, then nothing else needs to be done. If other security solutions in EMS E5 are relevant, then it is recommended to get the licensing via Microsoft 365 Enterprise. Otherwise, go with the standalone subscription.

Like other cloud-based security services in this book, the initial setup and configuration is performed in Azure automatically when you initialize it.

You will likely need to run a discovery and once the discovery is performed, the solution will determine all cloud applications in the environment. If historic information is needed, then manual upload of the traffic logs is performed. Also, based on the requirements automatic log uploads are setup. Sanctioned applications are connected directly via application connectors.

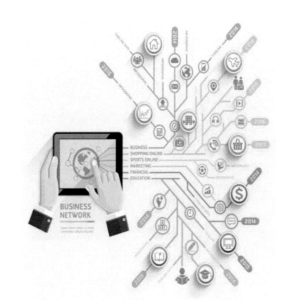

Reports generated from the discovery along with the Risk Assessment report are discussed with the customer to understand the current state of the environment.

Then, the policies are configured for the environment. The configurations are setup based on two approaches. First, based on the cloud applications discovered, the recommended policies are suggested for the known and most used applications. Secondly, the capabilities of the solution are discussed with the customer and then they decide what kind of control is needed based on their environment, internal security policies and custom applications. The user acceptance criteria may also be decided and documented for testing of the solution once configurations are complete.

Once the Cloud App Security solution is deployed and configured, the tests are performed simulating most common scenarios related to unusual user behavior, anomalies and security breaches. The tests are also performed from the agreed upon user acceptance criteria.

A typical project will also involve a knowledge-sharing workshop for the users within the organization on how to monitor and track the applications using Microsoft Cloud App Security portal and how to take actions based on various alerts on day-to-day basis.

The CASB does not need a client, will be mostly invisible to the end user if they are acting in a normal fashion. I raise these points because you are likely going to be able to deploy this in the enterprise in a few weeks, configure the app connectors and setup some additional policies in another couple of weeks.

8.4 The questions

- What is our current O365 license set and will we have to buy more for this?
- What are the network appliances, we are planning to target, from which the traffic logs will be collected?
- What are the locations and time zones from which the logs should be collected to get the most comprehensive insights into the environment?
- What historic logs and age limits should we analyze using manual upload into the solution?
- Which applications should be connected to the Cloud App Security solution?
- What different policies should be configured to provide better control?
- What behavior should be considered abnormal in the environment?
- What action should be taken when an alert is generated in the environment for each of the policy violations?
- What training in needed for the help desk in terms of file blocking?
- Do we need to communicate this tool to HR?

8.5 The mind map

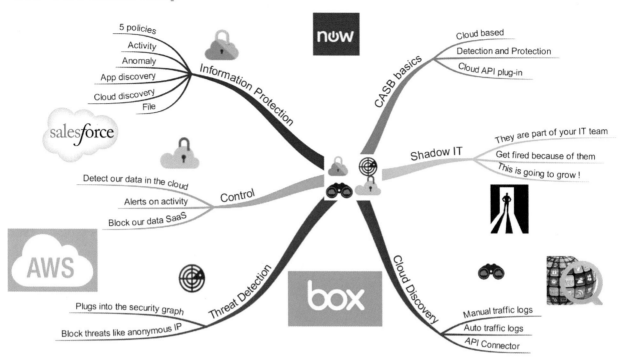

Notes:

9.0 AZURE MULTI FACTOR AUTHENTICATION (MFA)

What is the problem that Azure MFA is trying to solve?

A username and password combination (something you know) is a very weak authentication model, adding an additional layer like (something you have) a code sent to your phone increases the security dramatically.

USER | MFA protects your user account by adding an additional layer of security to the logon. Having a password, with a code that is sent to a PIN protected mobile means I have to physically have the phone to login. **This is a "Protection" tool.**

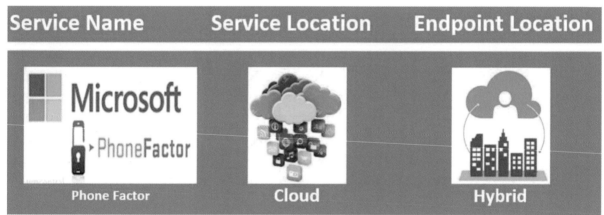

Service Name	Service Location	Endpoint Location
Phone Factor	Cloud	Hybrid

QR Code	Web location	Description
	https://www.youtube.com/watch?v=BqE63tg0oqU&feature=youtu.be	This is a short video on Azure MFA at the Born In The Cloud YouTube channel

9.1 Introduction

What is the best password in the world? … one that only works once! Multi Factor Authentication (MFA) or Two Factor Authentication (2FA) works by requiring another method usually involving a user's mobile phone. We love MFA because it makes the user login so much safer, but not needing it all the time is even better still.

A password that only worked once, was considered the gold standard. The largest IT companies in the world are now working on no passwords. Having a single login to all services, that does not involve any username /password combination, but instead uses technilogy like the facial recognition in "Windows Hello", to login to a device, and that authentication being used across your services is an example of this type of authentication. Soon advances in technology coupled with a spirit of cooperation between the IT giants who's services we consume will likely make the username and password a thing of the past. Being at the front of that authentication wave of change is paramount to any companies future data protection.

9.2 In detail

The username and password is, well let's face it, a liability. We must do something else to protect user accounts. MFA started out life as a physical "key fob" and to gain access to corporate resources you (quickly) entered your one time only code with your username and password. The rise of the smartphone allowed us to swap out the key fob for our phones and now we have a number of options for the authentication process.

There are two types of MFA, cloud based and in-house, both of which are licensed by your AAD license version. Certain roles in Azure admin get a MFA license for free but in general you must pay for it.

With MFA enabled we can present the user with several authentication options including;

- Being sent a code vis SMS
- Receiving an automated call and pressing # to complete the process
- Using a native smartphone app to generate the code
- Using the Azure Authentication App, we can receive a kind of SMS that asks us to accept the authentication request

Azure Multi-Factor Authentication

As we mentioned in chapter 5 on AAD-IP entering an MFA code all the time is a pretty laborious process. We really recommend having a user complete the registration for MFA to use it in conjunction with the enabling of AAD-IP.

Once the user is registered they can choose how they want the MFA to happen. We have several options with this;

- Make it a prerequisite for every login
- Let AAD-IP make the challenge where necessary

The Application Password

It's important to note that if you enforce MFA on our users, then Outlook and Skype for Business on every device will be prompted to perform an MFA, but they can't. To get around this you need to enter something called an Application Password. If you own several devices, this is inconvenient, this is exasperated when it involves thousands of users, with 2-4 devices. The best solution of all is to enable "modern authentication" on your O365 tenant, but this does require Office 2013 at the very least.

QR Code	Web location	Description
	https:// account.activedirect ory.windowsazure.c om/ AppPasswords.aspx	Handy link to the application password self service page

Receiving an email is our least preferred method of MFA, if your laptop was snatched from your table at a restaurant with you logged in, you typically have your email accounts in Outlook and so the MFA code with be sent to an email address that is accessible from the laptop☺.

9.3 The project

When we think about deploying MFA we need to ask if this is going to protect in-houses resources, cloud based resources or both. If you just want to use MFA to protect your cloud- based resources like Office 365 or Azure based resources, then you can use Microsoft's MFA cloud based service. It's very easy to setup and the user onboarding is pretty self-explanatory. It is very possible that your IT team could set this up, end users could register for it, and start to use it with no support at all. We absolutely recommend using MFA for end users, just use it in conjunction with Azure Active Directory Identity Protection covered in Chapter 5. This has the added advantage of being protected by MFA without needing application password for Skype and Outlook on everything.

verification options (learn more)

Methods available to users:
- ☑ Call to phone
- ☑ Text message to phone
- ☑ Notification through mobile app
- ☑ Verification code from mobile app

As we have already discussed that the user can do all the authentication via a phone (it does not even have to be a smart phone) and so there is no special equipment needed to getting a user up and running.

In terms of using MFA to protect in-house or IaaS based cloud resources (in any cloud provider) we typically use something like a Remote Desktop Gateway server and a Phone Factor server working in tandem. The RDP instance provides the application or desktop access, but to get to it there is an MFA prompt in addition to the usual username and password. We configure the RDS server to require RADIUS authentication from the MFA server. Deploying an RDP gateway (usually in clusters for high availability) might be a few days but no more. The Phone Factor server is downloaded from Microsoft, gets installed and is configured to prompt for an MFA logon before getting access to published resources. There is no doubt that this is more likely a week to configure and test, but overall it's a pretty minor task set.

Getting started with MFA is not that much of a challenge and we have both the cloud and in-house logins covered. With the Azure based MFA user option, you can enable it on a per user basis and on-boarding people in small groups will reduce the impact. For most organizations getting started in terms of the knowledge gathering, design and high level deployment of MFA for both cloud and in-house would take less than four weeks.

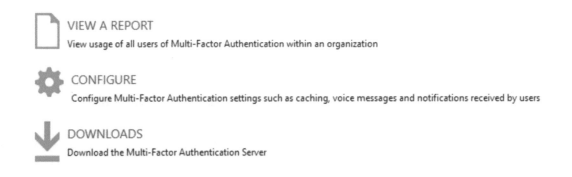

VIEW A REPORT
View usage of all users of Multi-Factor Authentication within an organization

CONFIGURE
Configure Multi-Factor Authentication settings such as caching, voice messages and notifications received by users

DOWNLOADS
Download the Multi-Factor Authentication Server

Of all the authentication options for MFA the two we find most user friendly are firstly using the Azure Authenticator App, that can send a form of SMS message that you accept, or to receive a phone call and press the hash key. Both methods are fast and the least intrusive options. The 6-digit code comes into the SMS notification screen of my iPhone and I always try and enter it before it disappears, and I have to unlock the phone. It's clunky experiences like this that make the other options a lot more appealing.

9.4 The questions

- Do we have a MFA solution in place right now?
- Can we protect on-premises and cloud-based resources with it?
- How will we on-board users?
- What training is needed for the helpdesk to support this?
- What if someone loses their phone or its stolen?
- Can we deploy separate physical MFA devices?
- Is there a way to spoof the MFA process?
- Does this integrate with our ADFS solution?
- How will we manage application passwords?
- Will we use this in conjunction with AAD-IP?

9.5 The mind map

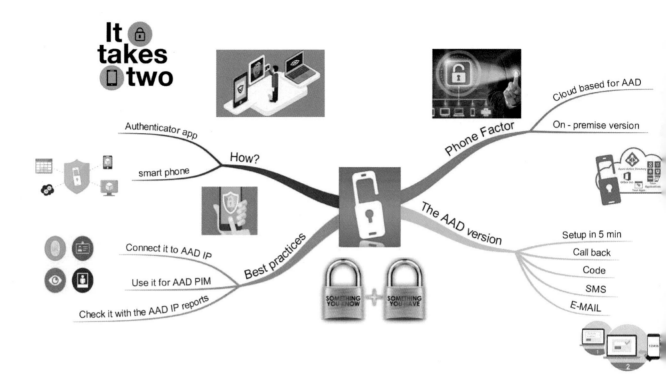

Notes:

10.0 AZURE INFORMATION PROTECTION (AIP)

What is the challenge that Azure Information Protection is trying to solve?

Azure Information Protection (AIP) protects documents on your endpoint, at rest, in the data center and when sent outside your network. AIP can apply policies and labelling to your documents based on keywords or number combinations. AIP will work on metadata in the documents stored locally on endpoints, file servers, Dropbox or in SharePoint, to name but a few. This is an essential tool if you are trying to address the **EU's 'GDPR** directive', as a user could 'revoke' access to the file from that point on.

Protect Document	Azure Information Protection will protect your data inside your corporate network on your devices, outside your network on your devices and on BYOD or non-company owned or controlled devices. **This is a "Protection" tool.**

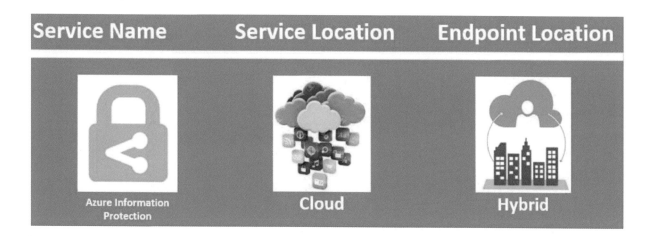

Service Name	Service Location	Endpoint Location
Azure Information Protection	Cloud	Hybrid

QR Code	Web location	Description
	https://www.youtube.com/channel/UCYmeOeI3sC_oXXE4VL4X8JQ	This is a short video on AIP at the Born In The Cloud YouTube channel

10.1   Introduction

AIP offers your organization 3 main data protection features;

Firstly, we can set policies that will control and define how user classify sensitive information like credit cards, social security numbers and health records for example.

Secondly, we can create a catch all net that will automatically detect sensitive information even if the user has not labeled it correctly.

Lastly, we can setup protection policies that prevent data sharing of documents by restricting the ability to print, forward or even view the document in a screen sharing application like Skype for Business or GoToMeeting for example. If you are using O365, all the underlying infrastructure is being secured for you by Microsoft. All the data however that you produce, the World Docs, emails, Excel spreadsheets, it is your responsibility to provide the protection, and Azure Information Protection is your tool to help you do exactly that.

In the image below you can see the default labeling of AIP, and we have added an additional label for "Medical Records"

Configure labels for this policy and order them by sensitivity level

LABEL NAME	DESCRIPTION	POLICY	MARKING	PROTECTION	
Personal	For personal use only. Thi	Global			...
Public	This information can be u	Global			...
Internal	This information includes	Global	✓		...
Confidential	This data includes sensitiv	Global	✓	paul keely - Confidential	...
▶ Secret	This data includes highly	Global	✓		...
Sensitivity		Global	✓	paul keely - Confidential View Only	...
Medical Records	This protection will be ap	Global	✓	paul keely - Confidential View Only	...

Protecting your data on any device, on any network in any location is a must have.

Having the ability to label and auto label is a great leap forward.

Lastly allowing the end user to review and revoke access brings us full circle.

10.2   In detail

AIP is a merger of two products, Rights Management Server (RMS) and Secure Islands (a company that Microsoft bought in 2015). There are two types of RMS, Microsoft RMS that is the on-premises version, and Azure RMS the SaaS based Azure version. AIP gives you the ability to create and apply policies in Azure, that can then get applied to document's irrespective of their location. The RMS template will control the rights a user has to a file, for example the policy may restrict the user's permissions to view only and some will allow more control.

From the end user's perspective, AIP starts off either with an agent deployed to their device, or by just using the native capabilities of Office and Windows. The AIP client will add a new labeling toolbar to their Office applications, and will add two buttons to their Office toolbar ribbon. To really use AIP the client is the best user experience.

The labeling feature allows you to assigning a default label, ("Internal" is the default label) and the user can select several different labels that will apply different types of RMS template. We can create a custom label like "Medical Records" and in this label, will can search for words like "Patient", or "Blood Type". When a user saves a document with either of these words, the file will be automatically saved with the label of "Medical Records" and the associated policy applied.

Once the document is ready to be shared, the user selects "Share Protected" from the toolbar, and AIP gets ready to share the file in an email, and we can then select the users to share it with.

When a user receives a protected document, they may need the RMS client to open and work with that document depending on the device in use. The important thing is that they must sign in to the Azure Information Protection service.

At the start of this book you will find the Microsoft security phase, "Protect, Detect & Respond. AIP is a protection service. So, when we say protecting the document what does that mean? When the RMS document is emailed, the recipients either inside or outside your organization will have restrictions applied like read-only, do not forward, do not print etc.

When an RMS protected, document is open on someone's device, depending on the policy, they will not be able to screen share the document with a conferencing tool like Skype for Business, or any other desktop sharing application. If they take a tool like "OneNote" and they use the "Screen Clipping" tool it will not be enabled and it is not possible to digitally copy that document, yes you could photograph the document with a smart-phone but that is something that is hard to stop.

Once the document has been sent and is out in the wild, the owner will receive an email with a link to a portal to view the status of the document. From the portal, we can view the number of users and number of times the document was accessed, the timeline and the location. At any point, the owner can recall the document and block all access to it no matter where it is and who has it.

Following on from the example above, where we added "Medical Records", you can see below the "Conditions" that will be checked for when a document is saved. Once one of the conditions is found in the document we will apply extra security to it.

Configure conditions for automatically applying this label

If any of these conditions are met, this label is applied

CONDITION NAME	OCCURRENCES
Medical Records	1
Blood Type	1
Patient Name	1

+ Add a new condition

The news is full of stories of "leaked" documents, stolen patents and important documents in the wrong hands. When we were writing this book, we had no fears when mailing a soft copy to anyone because AIP was protecting the document for us.

When creating a new label, it's possible to search for a set of built in conditions. Built-in conditions include fields such as credit card, IBAN, SWIFT or SSN.

10.3   The project

Deploying AIP has several elements, and there is quite a bit to it. We typically break this project down into 3 phases;

- The backend cloud design, configuration, and implementation
- The agent deployment
- The end user training and support

The backend cloud design, configuration and implementation
During this phase, you would identify the labels you want to use and custom labels you may need to add. Configure the RMS templates and do some testing with a pilot. Expect to spend a week or two identifying what the business needs are, initial testing and the pilot role out.

The agent deployment
Ideally, the agent needs to go to every device that wants to open an AIP protected document, laptops, desktops and mobile (Windows 10 and Office 2016 will get by without an agent, but iPhones etc. need the agent). You are going to need a configuration deployment tool like System Center Configuration Manager and Intune, or some other combination like LANDesk and Airwatch. Get the agent out as soon as you initiate the project, they are not very big but better to start the process sooner than later. Preparing the package is not a big deal but plan for 2-3 days for testing and monitoring the deployment.

The end user training and support
Something as simple as a Word doc, or a short video for 2-3 min should be enough to educate end users on what is involved.   When you receive a protected email, it arrives with a link to instructions, on what to do if the recipient does not have the agent installed, or if you are not AIP on-boarded. A few days for the training materials should be enough here. You are going to have to perform an initial end user education on the project so that they know that it's all about to happen. The fact that end users are going to interact with this in everyday life means it's going to have more risk than some of the other projects.

Expect 2-4 weeks to set labels and templates, and then 2-6 weeks to pilot this with different user groups and use cases. Any project that interacts with how users send, receive and work with Office documents needs to be "eased" into.

This image clearly shows the power of AIP. Firstly, the document MED5.docx has been revoked, it was viewed in both Europe and the US, and there were five attempts to read it that failed. It also shows the user account that was denied access.

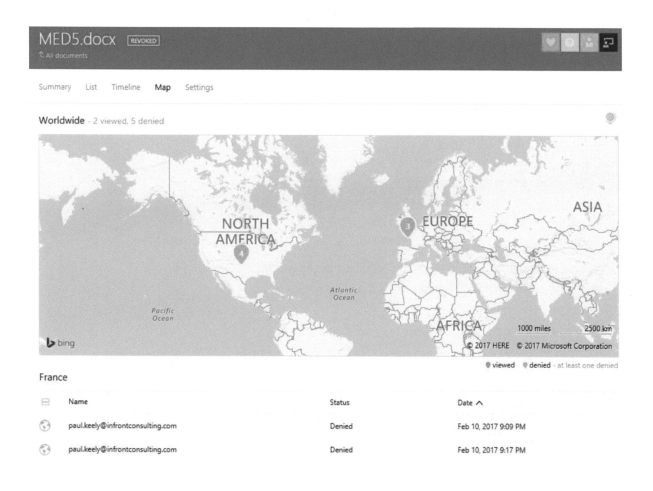

Will users feel that all this security is a lack of trust towards them, or that we are under non-stop attack? Quite likely, but we need to assure them that the steps we are taking, will make life as easy and secure as possible. We can allow them to "declassify" or use no labels; and they do not have to protect all documents. We have found that this project does result in an increase in help desk calls as people send mails that can't be opened. Microsoft is

working hard on updates to this suite that will include server side decryption and would negate the need for the client, and open the service up to 1 time only password access scenarios.

10.4   The questions

- Do we have a current information protection tool?
- Who will we deploy this to?
- Is it going enterprise wide?
- Who will the pilot group be?
- What will the success criteria for the pilot be?
- What are the default policies?
- What labels do we need?
- What custom words do we need to search for?
- What are the settings we are going to apply to our labels?
- How are we going to deploy the AIP client?
- How will we get it to mobile devices?
- How will we educate our end user on the tool?
- What do we need to do with our helpdesk to support this tool?
- Do we have any legal or compliance requirements for our data?
- How can we monitor the service?
- What if people can't access an RMS document externally?

> In this chapter we claim that you need a client for RMS, and its not 100% true. Modern OS's and apps like Windows 10 and Office 365 have built in RMS capabilities, no client needed. The fact is that the user experience is greatly enhanced with the AIP client as it allows us to share the document easily, and if we don't need to share the document then we didn't need the RMS protection in the first place.

10.5   The mind map

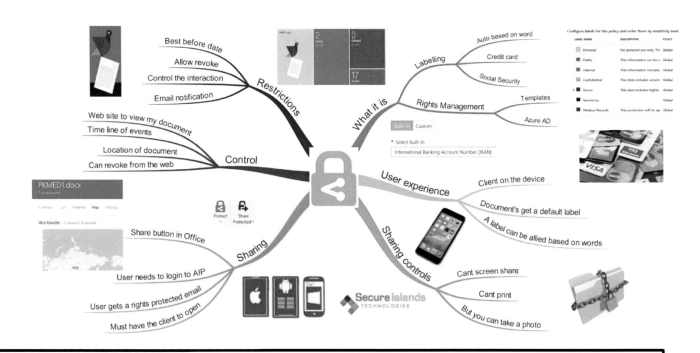

Notes:

11.0 MOBILE DEVICE MANAGEMENT (MDM)

What is the problem that Mobile Device Management is trying to solve?

The mobile revolution has already happened, smartphones are utterly ubiquitous, tablets have lagged the smartphone but are still popular and many employees get laptops that are very mobile (the new slimmer SSD laptop can actual be resting on the lap without the need for some insulating product from NASA to shield one's legs from the heat!). All of this poses a great security challenge to the three areas that this book focuses on, the user, the device and the data.

Device	Protect Document	*Intune deploys a client to your endpoints to help manage them with software update, AV updates, security settings, Applications and so on.* **This is a "Protection", and "Response" tool.**

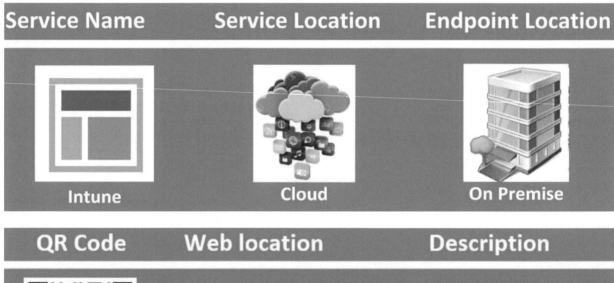

Service Name	Service Location	Endpoint Location
Intune	Cloud	On Premise

QR Code	Web location	Description
	https://www.youtube.com/watch?v=XBMJZnUMpx8	Intune video on the Microsoft Mechanics YouTube page

11.1   Introduction

Microsoft's MDM solution is called Intune, and it's a cloud-based service that can manage the 3-main phone/tablet types, iPhone, Android, and Windows. It can also manage Windows and Mac devices like laptops and desktops that are inside or outside the corporate network.

11.2   In detail

Microsoft made a pretty bold decision a few years ago when instead of running something like System Center Configuration Manager in the cloud and calling it an MDM solution, they wrote a cloud-based MDM solution from scratch.

The result is an MDM solution that is enterprise grade, and capable of meeting most corporate mobility control requests. Intune can be deployed as a cloud only service or as a hybrid service connecting to System Center Configuration Manager.

It's very important that Intune (and these Azure based tools) are deployed under the same Azure tenant so that we can integrate authentication from Azure AD and the health of devices can count towards a device health attestation.

After an Intune subscription is enabled, we can access it as a standalone service and with a couple of onboarding policies will have you ready to start importing mobile clients, and downloading the client for the likes of Windows 10 etc.

Microsoft basically split the Intune feature set into 2 large groupings. Mobile Device Management (MDM) and Mobile App Management (MAM). To protect a device, you need to start off with the agent deployment. So, let's look at the features associated with each of the groupings.

MDM feature sets

- Inventory the devices hardware and software
- Deploy software
- Deploy software updates
- Configure security settings (PIN length on a phone for example) Deploy security certificates (VPN's, Wi-Fi, etc.)
- Restrict access to corporate resources to predefined apps (Outlook, OneDrive etc.)
- Perform remote administration of the device (device wipe, etc.)
- Anti-Malware definition updates

MAM feature sets include

- Publishing mobile apps to employees
- Configuring apps
- Controlling how corporate data is used and shared in mobile apps
- Removing corporate data from mobile apps
- Updating mobile apps
- Reporting on mobile app inventory
- Tracking mobile app usage

MDM is an essential pillar in your security stance and gets more important the more mobile your workforce becomes. Having an MDM tool that plugs into the rest of your Azure focused security estate means you can leverage data points being pulled from throughout your organization.

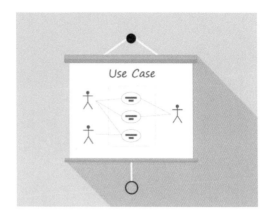

Let's look at some of the common use cases for Intune.

1. Protect on-premises email and data
2. Protecting Office 365 email
3. Facilitate secure BYOD to employees
4. Issue secure corporate-owned phones
5. Provide limited-use shared tablets
6. Restrict access to O365 from unmanaged public devices.

1 Exchange Server on-premises can connect with Intune's "Conditional Access" settings that require a device to be "Enrolled", or no access will be approved.

2 In Office 365 we can ask for security compliance requirements like MFA, Intune Enrollment, managed apps, device PIN, etc.

3 Intune supports BYOD in that we can control features like "managed apps" enforcing the use of Outlook, and we can control the security features that Outlook will support.

4 The mobile enrollment process can be greatly reduced from an end user perspective by bulk provisioning with the Apple Device Enrollment Program.

5 The bulk provisioning of "single line-of-business" apps pre-configured. This support covers iOS and Android.

6 What if we want to limit access to our resources when the access requests are coming from untrusted, unmanaged sources then we can configure settings to limit email access to devices that are managed by only corporate- owned devices.

11.3   The project

Depending on the size and complexity of your organization deploying Intune could vary in duration and effort but it's more than likely one of the longer deployments you are likely to tackle as part of this book. Any project that looks to deploy agents out to your devices by its nature faces challenges like resources being unavailable, the cooperation of the end user and the impact of deploying security changes to people's devices.

For even a pretty small enterprise of 2000 end points it's very likely that deploying Intune is going to be a relatively large project. The first question you need to answer is are you going to go for cloud-only or integrate into SCCM also known as hybrid mode. If you already have SCCM deployed, and you want a single pane of glass then hybrid mode is your likely path.

Intune requires an agent on every device it's going to manage. Deploying to Windows devices like laptops and desktops is basically an agent with a certificate. Once the agent is deployed the device is managed and from that point on you can group is and apply security to it. iOS and Android devices need the Intune App and this will allow the device to be enrolled.

Any project that requires an agent on all devices requires some thought and planning. If that agent then prevents access to applications and resources then we are in another level of potential help desk calls, and so a good pilot group for Intune is critical.

As Intune is a cloud-based service there is none of the typical backend configuration, and you can onboard and configure 2000 devices in a few weeks, you still need to plan for testing phases for the big phases like;

Application Deployment

Software Updates

Security Settings

11.4 The questions

- Do we have an MDM tool in place now?
- What are the risks to the business of deploying this tool?
- What are the risks if we do not deploy this tool?
- What is the business case for this tool?
- Will this project be "felt" or visible to the general end user population?
- Will our licensing changes mean we are paying for 2 MDM products?
- Will this be cloud or hybrid based service?
- What are the business impacts of deploying Intune to existing iOS clients in the field?
- What is the impact of deploying this to new iOS devices?
- What features of Intune do we need to deploy for compliance?
- Do we have a corporate standard security policy for mobile devices?
- Will we be deploying 3rd party apps through Intune?
- Will we be deploying in-house apps through Intune?
- What inventory do we need from our devices?
- Will we perform remote device wipe, and if so are there legal implications for this?

11.5   The mind map

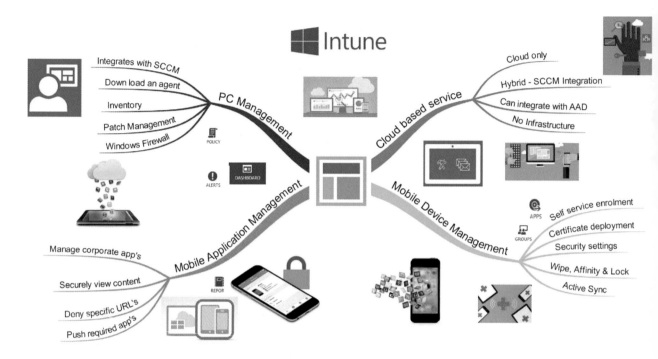

Intune

PC Management
- Integrates with SCCM
- Down load an agent
- Inventory
- Patch Management
- Windows Firewall

POLICY

ALERTS

DASHBOARD

Cloud based service
- Cloud only
- Hybrid - SCCM Integration
- Can integrate with AAD
- No Infrastructure

Mobile Application Management
- Manage corporate app's
- Securely view content
- Deny specific URL's
- Push required app's

REPOR

Mobile Device Management

APPS

GROUPS
- Self service enrolment
- Certificate deployment
- Security settings
- Wipe, Affinity & Lock
- Active Sync

Notes:

12.0 OPERATIONS MANAGEMENT SUITE (OMS)

What is the problem that Operations Management Suite (or OMS) is trying to solve?

OMS is trying to manage and monitor workloads, in-house or in any cloud, running on any platform. It collects monitoring data from your infrastructure, and raises alerts for any suspicious activities. It also allows you to take automated actions when an alert is raised. It further allows you to replicate and protect the workloads for disaster recovery.

Device	User	OMS looks for unauthorized access or compromised accounts. It also checks for devices with insufficient protection, authentication issues or any other security issues. **This is a Protection, Detection and Response tool.**

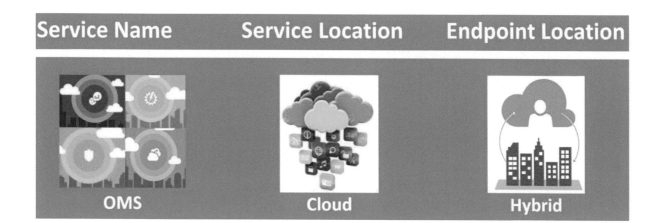

Service Name	Service Location	Endpoint Location
OMS	Cloud	Hybrid

QR Code	Web location	Description
	https://www.youtube.com/watch?v=8qzH85zmpC8&feature=youtu.be	This is a short video on Azure OMS at the Born In The Cloud YouTube channel

12.1   Introduction

Infrastructure can grow at a very fast pace. When we introduce cloud into the equation, you need a unified solution to monitor and manage your ever-growing hybrid workload's. Operations Management Suite (or OMS) provides a suite of solutions for managing, monitoring and protecting workloads. These solutions include:

- **Security and Compliance** – to secure and audit your datacenter with full visibility to all security data and with advanced threat detection
- **Log Analytics** – providing Insights and analytics to monitor and troubleshoot application and infrastructure issues
- **Automation and Desired State Configurations** – to increase control with automation and provide configuration management
- **Protection and Recovery** – to ensure data protection with cloud Backup and Disaster Recovery (DR).

OMS really is the hybrid management tool. Monitoring across environments even with no VPN in-place, just internet access.

While we are just focusing on the monitoring component here, the automation and DR components work equally well across all locations, but are a little out of scope.

12.2   In detail

OMS provides visibility and control across your hybrid cloud with simplified management and security across clouds and platforms. It is a cloud native and cost effective solution supporting Windows or Linux running in public, private or hybrid scenarios.

OMS provides various solutions to centralize and control your enterprise server security and allows you to perform more intelligent and effective threat detection.

The Security and Audit gallery solution, is a unique service in OMS which provides:

- A comprehensive view of your organization's IT security posture using built-in search queries.

- Faster investigation and resolution of risks
- Identifying configuration changes to pinpoint unexpected modifications

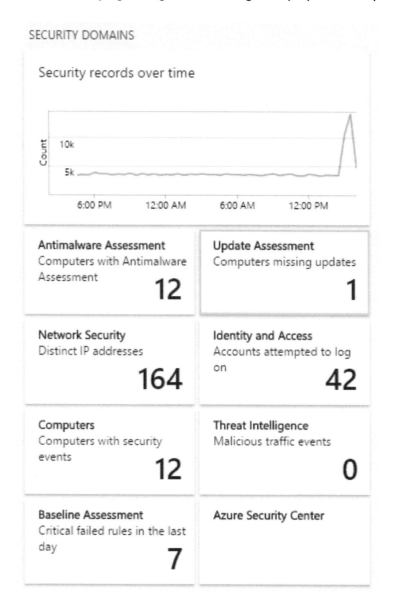

The "Security and Audit" page provides all the graphics we are going to see in this chapter.

The "Security Domains" section provides you with an excellent overview of the security health of your servers.

The "Identity and Access" page gives us an amazing insight into our logon attempts.

We also get a link to "Azure Security Center", where you can pivot straight to that portal.

Using custom built or "out-of-the-box" solutions gets actionable insights for IT operations and security. Leverage OMS's Security and Audit dashboard to gain high-level insights into the security state of any monitored environment. You can get insights via four sections of Security and Audit:

1. **Security Domains** – View security records over time

2. **Notable Issues** – Get an at-a-glance view of security issues requiring attention. E.g., suspicious user activity or compromised accounts. View computers with insufficient protection and authentication issues.
3. **Threat Intelligence** – Visualize and track any malicious traffic.
4. **Common Security Queries** – Your go-to place for getting answers to most common security questions

View data related to:

- Antimalware assessment
- Update assessment
- Network security
- Identity and Access
- Workloads
- Baseline Assessment
- Suspicious executables

> **OMS has color coded "out of the box solutions" that include a large amount of security data. The "Security and Audit" tools offer security insights that are often worryingly eye opening.**

Once you identify an issue, you can simply drill down to view details and related data for any security threat or issue. You can even select a particular instance of the event to see its details.

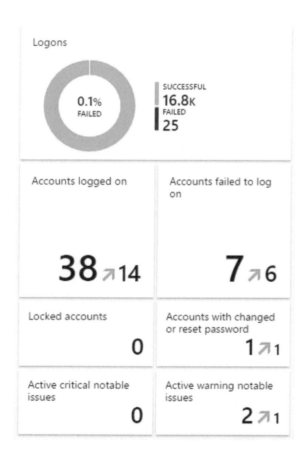

The "Identity Posture" page gives us incredible insight into our account information.

When you enable this tool in your environment the first thing that will shock you is the amount of failed login attempts for the "Administrator" account and many others. You need to go and rename this account on all servers.

You can visualize malicious traffic via maps showing incoming and outgoing traffic. OMS uses cloud scale resources to unlock new faster ways to solve and prevent problems to streamline operations. The OMS portal provides a holistic view of all your managed resources across multiple clouds and platforms. It provides assessment for your critical deployments, configurations, and applications such as:

- SQL
- Active Directory
- Configurations
- System Update
- Resource Utilization
- Change Tracking
- Alert Management

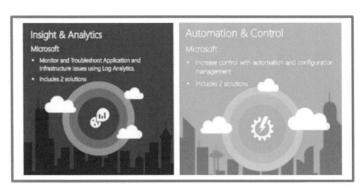

OMS gives us the ability to monitor the security of your Windows and Linux servers in AWS, IBM or Azure, combined with your data centers and remote offices. As well as server monitoring it will also monitor web apps and infrastructure. The OMS suite has an automation engine that can run recovery or security configuration settings in response to alerts. It can also patch your servers.

OMS helps you to proactively resolve issues before they become problems, using alert management in combination with Azure Automation. Deploy automated and orchestrated tasks to run against workloads across the environment.

Backup and Recovery in OMS allows you to easily protect applications and data from all your machines. With Site Recovery, you can orchestrate replication, failover, and recovery of workloads and apps. This ensures availability from a secondary location if your primary location goes down. This solution within OMS helps you protect against any potential Ransomware threats as well.

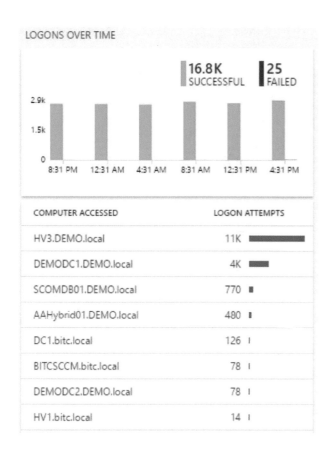

In this image, you can see the top number of logins to servers. If you are looking for a smoking gun, then 2 servers with 15000 logins and others servers at less than 1000 is enough to spark some interest.

12.3   The project

An OMS project starts with identifying the infrastructure and the workloads which should be monitored and managed. Log Analytics (along with Security and Audit related solutions) is agent based. The agent for OMS is pushed in either a manual or automated fashion.

You can also have System Center Operations Manager (or SCOM) in-house configured as connected source for OMS. It can then send the data to OMS which can also be used for monitoring.

Once the agent is in place or the connectivity with SCOM is setup, OMS starts receiving the data. With this in place, you can build dashboards for day to day reporting. This phase depends on what kind of dashboards you are looking for and how many metrics you want in each of the dashboards. A typical dashboard can contain data, graphs and pie charts pertaining to questions like:

- How many computers are missing security or critical updates?
- How many overall active critical issues V's warning are present?
- How many accounts failed to logon?
- Terminated remote sessions that have not been logged off.
- Distinct malicious IP addresses accessed.
- Change or reset password attempts made.
- Failed account login attempts.
- Security activities on specific mission-critical workloads.
- Event Log errors by Event ID for a specific Event Log.
- Event Log errors by Computer.
- List of all the systems which have been up for more than 180 days.
- Servers running low on Memory or CPU.

You can generate alerts based on any criteria on the data collected by OMS. If you also want to take an automated remediation action, then you can connect the alerts to Azure Automation. This can execute tasks automatically based on the issue generated.

If the automation is complex or is not available from the community, then development effort will be needed to build this custom automation in Azure. For many scenarios, there is a Microsoft or community provided automation runbook available which can cut down the development efforts and overall time to delivery.

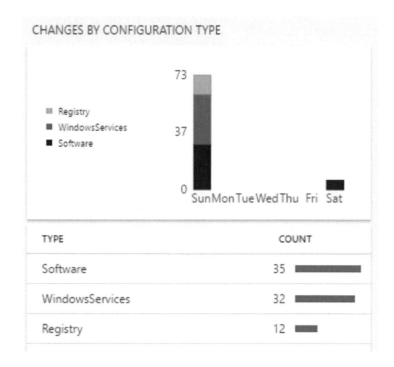

CHANGES BY CONFIGURATION TYPE

■ Registry
■ WindowsServices
■ Software

TYPE	COUNT	
Software	35	▬▬▬▬▬
WindowsServices	32	▬▬▬▬▬
Registry	12	▬▬

There are several key questions we need to be answered as part of our Key Security Indictors (KSI), are we missing security patches, do we have AV and of course what changes have been made to my systems regarding files, application, and services. OMS is the perfect pace for all of this, in one great dashboard.

Azure Site Recovery (ASR)
ASR is the DR component of the OMS suite. It is a replication tool that replicates in-house servers to Azure.   A recovery vault is set up in Azure and a management server is configured in-house. This server in-house works as an intermediary and replicates any number of servers from the local datacenter to the cloud.

First, the initial replication of the server is done via ASR and a copy of the production server is replicated over to Azure from which a server can be created in the cloud. After this initial replication has completed, only delta changes for the server are replicated, optimizing bandwidth consumption and cost. The overall estimate of the time that it will take for the replication to finish can be calculated using the Microsoft Excel-based tool Capacity Planner. The factors affecting the time taken are:

- Total disk size
- Number of disks
- Data change rate on the disks, etc.

The replication changes are just held in a BLOB storage account in the cloud, there is no VM, in the event of an emergency the VM will be spun up from the BLOB storage and only then do you start to pay for compute resources. ASR allows you to restore to a point in time so it also offers protection against potential security threats like Ransomware etc.

As so many attacks take advantage of software updates, getting visibility to your update compliance state is made very easy through OMS.

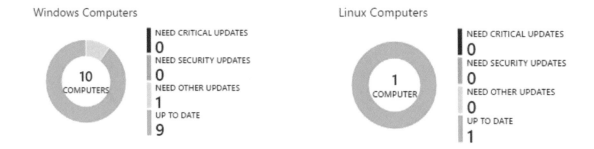

12.4   The questions

- What are the servers which need to be monitored via OMS?
- Is this going to Windows and Linux?
- Do you have existing System Center Operations Manager deployment in-house to monitor your infrastructure? Do you want to connect it with OMS?
- How do you want the monitoring agent to be deployed on target workloads in your infrastructure?
- How many metrics do you want to see in the dashboard?
- What are the metrics you are interested in viewing reports for?
- What kind of Event Log errors you want to monitor?
- What Performance counters you want to monitor?
- What are the security questions for which you want the insights?
- What are the servers which are mission critical and needs to be protected?
- What is the size of each server that needs to be replicated and protected in the cloud?

We can gain insights into our security auditing dashboards.

Top User Logons with Administrator Privileges

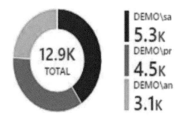

DEMO\sa
5.3k
DEMO\pr
4.5k
DEMO\an
3.1k

Top Remote Logons by Computer

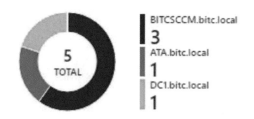

BITCSCCM.bitc.local
3
ATA.bitc.local
1
DC1.bitc.local
1

Top Remote Logons by User

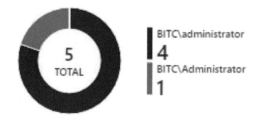

BITC\administrator
4
BITC\Administrator
1

All Security Events

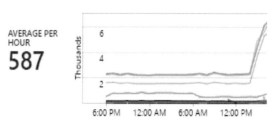

AVERAGE PER HOUR
587

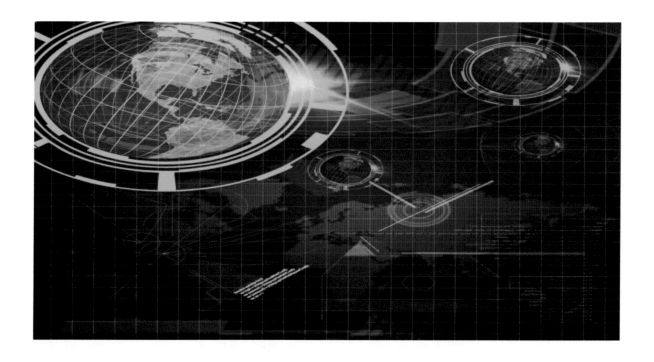

12.5 The mind map

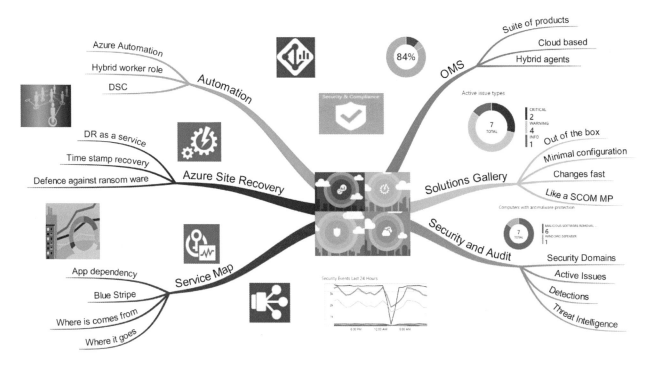

- Azure Automation
- Hybrid worker role
- DSC
  - **Automation**

- DR as a service
- Time stamp recovery
- Defence against ransom ware
  - **Azure Site Recovery**

- App dependency
- Blue Stripe
- Where is comes from
- Where it goes
  - **Service Map**

84%

Security & Compliance

- Suite of products
- Cloud based
- Hybrid agents
  - **OMS**

Active issue types

7 TOTAL
CRITICAL 2
WARNING 4
INFO 1

- Out of the box
- Minimal configuration
- Changes fast
- Like a SCOM MP
  - **Solutions Gallery**

Computers with antimalware protection

7 TOTAL
MALICIOUS SOFTWARE REMOVAL 6
WINDOWS DEFENDER 1

- Security Domains
- Active Issues
- Detections
- Threat Intelligence
  - **Security and Audit**

Security Events Last 24 Hours

Notes:

13.0 AZURE SECURITY CENTER (ASC)

What is the problem that Azure Security Center is trying to solve?

Azure Security Center gives you enhanced visibility and increased control over your Azure resources by helping you to prevent, detect, and respond to threats. With integrated security monitoring, policy management and implementation across your subscriptions resources. ASC will help you close the gaps that could be otherwise hard to find and protect your cloud-based environment with ease.

Device	App	*Azure Security Center really is the one stop tool for securing your cloud based resources. It will focus on VM's Networks, SQL and Data.* **This is a "Protection", "Detection" and "Response" tool.**

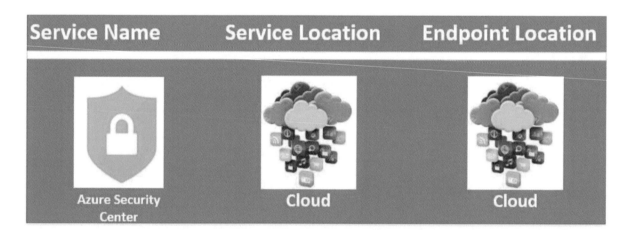

Service Name	Service Location	Endpoint Location
Azure Security Center	Cloud	Cloud

QR Code	Web location	Description
	https://www.youtube.com/watch?v=UWevJbusS_o	This is a short video on Azure Security Center at the Born In The Cloud YouTube channel

13.1   Introduction

Cloud makes it very easy for us to deploy resources with a few clicks. ARM templates allow us to deploy servers, apps, networking and all the supporting artifacts in-between. This all sounds great, but we all know that making it easy to deploy something means we deploy more and more. SQL sprawl was followed by VM sprawl and now we face cloud sprawl. While we want to make it easy to deploy to the cloud we must ensure that security is paramount in all phases.

The problem with sweeping statements like security is paramount is that like many things in IT, it's a lot easier said than done. Azure Security Center or ASC should be your first point of reference for Azure-based resources.

ASC is like having a security assessment performed in your environment; it just happens all the time. This tool set is so powerful and easy to use that it needs to part of every Azure IaaS and PaaS environment.

ASC has a detailed prevention policy, detailed recommendations and a list of alerts on each resource. It can plug into a centralized Security Information and Event Management (SIEM) systems like Q-RADAR and Eventhubs.

We view ASC as a "must have" security tool for cloud based resources. Not only does it help prevent soft targets in your cloud based infrastructure, it also allows you to remediate many of the issues, from right inside the console. If I deployed VM's without a network level firewall (NSG) it will identify the security weakness and allow us to either create a new NSG or deploy an existing NSG to your server.

13.2   In detail

ASC starts off with a dashboard that gives you an immediate view of your environmental security health. We always start off with this dashboard as it's an easy to understand, and super clear experience.

The ASC service is available to every subscription; you just need to switch it on or "opt in". It will offer protection to IaaS and PaaS because you have much more control (and responsibility) for the security of these environments. With a solution like O365 Microsoft, own the responsibility for securing the infrastructure and that is the fundamental difference.

ASC connects to the Intelligent Security Graph (from chapter 1) and allows for advanced threat detection capabilities. The detections include;

Threat detections – VM's having outbound traffic with known malicious IP address.

Behavioral Analytics – VM's doing something it's not supposed to, like file copies or sending/relaying emails.

Anomalies – VM doing something not normal like an increase in traffic to other VM's that far exceeds normal traffic.

Fusion – Joining alerts and events to build out an attack timeline.

The "prevention" screen shows the defense in depth of your VM's, Network, SQL, and Applications

Quick Start

To begin ASC, we use the quick start guide with 4 steps to help secure your environment.

The "Policy" setting allow us to apply a set of detection settings to an entire subscription, or at a specific resource group. In the policy, we chose what storage account to use to store the data and what policies we want to apply.

The "Recommendations" tab allows you to either view guidance on how to make the required changes or even better you can make the changes from right inside the console. You can deploy encryption to SQL drives, or enable endpoint protection for example.

From the "Security Health" view, you get an instant view of the security health of your cloud based resources. It will quickly let you see the "hot spots" in your VM estate, networks and applications.

The "Alerts View" allows you to see what the issues are, their count and severity. The alerts come with a great explanation on what to do to resolve them.

ASC is an "opt-in" services, meaning that it is available to all subscriptions, but you must enable it. It can be enabled right for your top level subscription, and then all resources will be protected. Another option is to focus this on the Resource Group. The prevention policy covers all the areas of ASC;

- VM
- Network
- Application
- SQL

Show recommendations for

System updates ❶	On	Off
OS vulnerabilities ❶	On	Off
Endpoint protection ❶	On	Off
Disk encryption	On	Off
Network security groups	On	Off
Web application firewall	On	Off
Next generation firewall	On	Off
Vulnerability Assessment	On	Off
Storage Encryption	On	Off
SQL auditing & Threat detection	On	Off
SQL Encryption	On	Off

The recommendations options allow us to investigate and remediate so many of the components that our applications depend on.

We can verify our system updates and AV. We can help secure data at rest with disk encryption.

We can secure our resources with several levels of defense in terms of local firewalls, network firewalls, and 3rd party firewalls.

Lastly, we can work to protect our SQL PaaS environments.

What a great tool!

ASC allows you to get right to the cause of the security issues in your environment. ASC can be accessed directly from the OMS security page.

In terms of how you can interact with and understand the security health of your cloud resources, you can also visualize this with Power BI.

13.3   The project

ASC is enabled on all subscriptions, but getting the advanced detections requires an upgrade to the standard tier, and that's it... well, it's not that simple. Enabling the service is a quick process but like lots of the other SaaS based projects in this book, you need to plan what are the actions steps needed in response to the alerts.

We usually take the approach of documenting the recommendations and what can be automated from the console versus what we need to take manual action on. It should be noted that some of the recommendations like apply a new firewall or network security group will need some thoughts and fore planning on the impacts on the current estate.

This is a SaaS-based product, for resources in the cloud, that can often be remediated by cloud-based automation, from within the tool. All of this means that this is fast to on-board and fast to get to terms with.

We usually plan a pilot phase for 2-4 weeks where we start with a design session on;

- Storage account usage
- Resource group settings
- Policy settings

We then look to;

- Enable the toolset
- Review the policies
- Review the issues and alerts from the pilot
- Develop an action and communication strategy for the resources

The goal of the pilot and the tool, in general is to resolve all critical issues as a starting point and then ideally move on to all resources being green in the console.

13.4 The questions

- How can we verify the compliance of our cloud-based resources?
- What other existing solutions do we have to provide the same services?
- How will the alerts be managed from this product?
- How will the recommendations be dealt with?
- Who will we escalate issues to?
- Can we report on the health of this solution?
- Can this be connected to Power BI to get us better overall insight into the environment?
- What is this going to cost us?
- What are the risks to the business of deploying this tool?
- What are the risks if we do not deploy this tool?
- What is the business case for this tool?
- Will this project be "felt" or visible to the general end user population?
- What training is needed for the helpdesk to support this?

13.5   The mind map

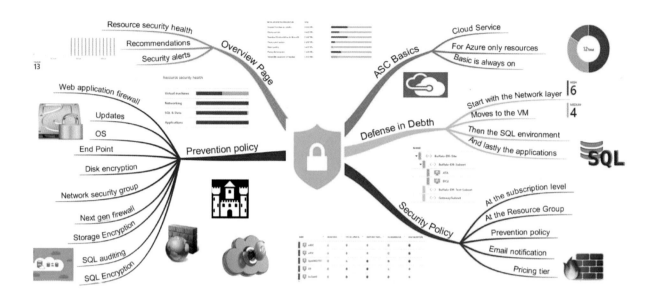

14.0 WINDOWS 10

What is the problem that Windows 10 is trying to resolve?

The clear majority of enterprises use a Windows endpoint either laptop or desktop. Windows 10 is trying to make the end user experience the safest and most secure it can be while not making this protection immediately visible to the end user.

Device	User	*Windows 10 is deployed to your endpoints.* **This is a "Protection" and "Detection" tool.**

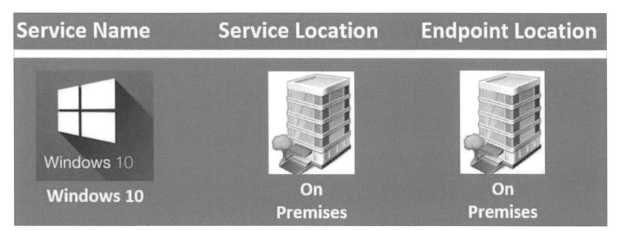

Service Name	Service Location	Endpoint Location
Windows 10	On Premises	On Premises

QR Code	Web location	Description
	https://channel9.msdn.com/ Series/Windows-10-Bites-for-Business/Windows-10-for-Enterprise-Empower-your-business-to-do-great-things	Windows 10 video on the Channel 9

14.1   Introduction

Windows 10 is Microsoft's most secure operating system yet, or at least you can choose to make it that way. Windows 10 allows us to prevent rootkits, pass the hash attacks and control applications that run on the device. Security was one of the leading pillars in the design matrix for Windows 10 and each of the major updates. One of the greatest challenges in the client management area has been attacks that happen before the OS has been loaded.

Our devices have been good at defending attacks with AV loaded into the OS, but what happens if your device has been infected during the boot process? What can give you early malware protection? Windows 10!

14.2   In detail

With the large number of Windows 10 security features, there is a lot to understand what is in focus when we talk about securing the endpoint. In this section, we are going to look at the features and make it as easy to understand as possible, so that you have a good starting point to discuss Windows 10. This chapter just by its very nature must go into more technical detail than almost any other. But saying that we will do our best to diagram this out in as clear and simple a process as we can so that the information may not be too boring.

Much of what we are going to cover here in terms of deploying and maintaining a secure Windows 10 endpoint brings so many of the technologies listed in the previous chapter's full circle.

We didn't discuss System Center Configuration Manager (SCCM) and chances are you already have it deployed as your configuration management system, but to give you some example of the upgrade and deployment user experience. When you deploy Windows 10 to an existing device via SCCM; the existing user's data will be captured and saved, existing Bitlocker drive encryption will be disabled, all network and devices settings captured. Now Windows 10 gets deployed, the drive gets encrypted, all your apps get installed, and the end user's data gets returned. The Windows 10 image can be patched every month so you don't have to wait during imaging for a patch cycle. Best of all, much if not all the security settings listed here (hardware permitting) can be applied, controlled, and reported upon. Windows 10, with SCCM/Intune, Windows Defender, and Windows Defender ATP is the sweet spot.

The Windows 10 security stance can be broken down into 3 main categories; We are going to look at each section in more detail below, but first, we are going to focus in a little bit more detail on Virtualization-based security (VBS) as this is critical to Windows 10.

Identity and Access Management

Windows Hello
Brute-force resistance
Credential Guard

Information Protection

Disk Encryption
Windows Information Protection

Threat Resistance

Virtualization-based security
Device Guard
Configurable code integrity
Measured boot and remote attestation

Virtualization-based security (VBS).

In VBS we deploy a small subset of the features of HyperV to your Windows 10 devices. We then place components like the Local Security Authority(LSA) into this secure hypervisor environment. This secure separation essentially means that someone with control over the system kernel, does not get access to the LSA. This means that attacks like pass the hash are made much more difficult (there is no publicly know way to perform this attack on a VBS enabled device at the moment)

With this model, we combine technologies like UIFI to maintain a secure boot process. We enable Early Learning Anti Malware to start scanning for malware well before the OS has finished loading and the AV agent starts.

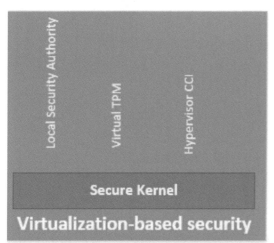

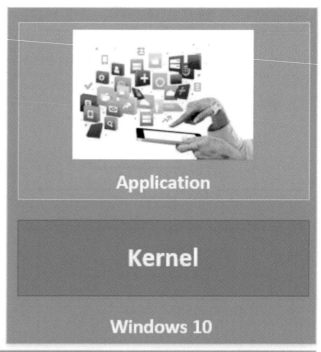

Identity and Access Management

Windows Hello
Brute-force resistance
Credential Guard

Windows Hello

Windows Hello is a 2FA/MFA solution. Windows Hello can scan your face, eyes or fingerprint. When your biometrics are identified, you get logged in. This is all built-in native technology that is simple and un-invasive. Windows Hello does require modern hardware.

Brute Force Resistance

Windows has long since had methods of "tar sanding" login attempts when a maximum number of failure attempts has been reached. Windows 10 takes this further by combining a TPM chip on the system, and restarting the device in a Bitlocker recovery mode.

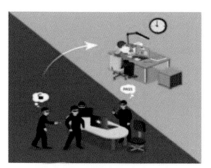

Credential Guard

Attacking a user's password with tools like Mimikatz allows an attacker to hack the password hash, and then use a "pass this hash" to move to other machines (lateral movement) and then look to get passwords from higher value accounts. Credential Guard prevents this using HyperV technology to separate out the Local Security Authority from the OS kernel.

Information Protection

Disk Encryption
Windows Information Protection

Disk Encryption

Disk encryption in the form of Bitlocker has been around for a long time, However Windows 10 has upped the game on it. On a new build, Bitlocker will only encrypt the space used, and not the whole drive. Bitlocker can store the pre-boot pin in the TPM chip, so there is no end user intervention for full SSO. Lastly we can store the key in MBAM enhanced security in our environment, if the device was encrypted outside the domain we can now escrow the key into MBAM on return.

Data Protection

Data Loss Protection (DLP) is a pretty serious concern to us all. This is one place were simple mistakes can leave data in the wrong hands. DLP usually works with Intune to enforce policies around how users interact with corporate data. We can encrypt data on both corporate and BYOD devices. We can remotely wipe corporate data, and leave personal data intact, and lastly we can even control the apps we want users to use when working with company data.

Threat Resistance

Virtualization-based security

Device Guard

Configurable code integrity

Measured boot and remote attestation

Hypervisor Code Integrity HVCI

VBS as discussed previously, is used here to help protect you from Zero Day exploits by ensuring that all code running in kernel mode is properly scoped, to control that the pre-boot drivers match the desired configuration.

Device Guard

Device Guard at its simplest form allows you to create "white lists" for the applications you want to allow run. This is similar to "App Locker" but it's much deeper. The code integrity (CI) template is a trust-nothing stance, called configurable code integrity (CCI).

Remote Device Attestation

Anti-malware and anti-virus software cannot protect the device during the boot process. The tools mentioned in the other sections like UIFI, secure boot, VBS etc. really help protect the boot process. But how do we know that this boot process was measured and is safe? With Remote Device Attestation that is exactly what we do, we verify the boot process, send this to a "device health cloud based attestation service". This health attestation can then be used by Intune for "conditional access" policies.

14.3   The project

Deploying a new Operating System to the entire estate is a big undertaking. Just deploying a Windows 10 image has a lot going on, but then planning and implementing these security features takes a lot of planning and understanding.

The project will follow these phases;

- Assess the current estate
- Design goals for the Windows 10
- Building the Windows image
- Configuring the application deployment
- Configuring the security settings
- Loading the user personal data

Assess the current estate
In this phase get a clear understanding of the current client estate in terms of hardware specs and requirements. With this assessment, you will know what your desired outcome is and what hardware refresh rates you are going to need. Microsoft has a new tool that plugs into OMS called upgrade analytics that can greatly help here.

Design Goals
In this phase, you need to identify the goals for the project. An important thing to consider is that if you want to deploy out the new security features listed above, you may only need this full feature set on remote workers and maybe some hardware swapping might save some costs on the refresh.

Building the Windows Image
In this phase, you will build and capture a Windows WIM, making sure you use the right version, removing the annoying built-in apps and adding company branding. The image needs to be tested and signed off.

Configuring the application deployment
Package, deploy and test the applications on the WIM.

Configuring the security settings
Build out a deployment strategy for;
- ➤ BIOS changes
- ➤ UIFE settings
- ➤ Secure Boot
- ➤ Credential Guard
- ➤ Device Guard
- ➤ Bitlocker settings

- ➢ Windows ATP agent
- ➢ SCCM/Intune agent
- ➢ App Locker policies
- ➢ AV settings
- ➢ Azure Information Protect agent
- ➢ Deploy the One Drive for Business settings

Loading the user's personal data
Load the User State Migration data to the new device

Expect to spend 10-20 weeks on the prepping, building and testing this process.

14.4   The questions

- What are the benefits to the business of moving to Windows 10?
- What are the risks to the business of adopting the technology as a security posture?
- Do we have an idea on the hardware refresh needed to support this?
- How much will the security strategy cost?
- Would it have helped us when we were attacked the last time?
- Will this increase our end-user training requirements?
- We have a lot of other security products in place do we need this migration?
- Do we have a client security policy or future desired end state?
- What is the end-to-end cost of the project going to be?
- What is the business case for this project and do we feel it's warranted?
- What team is going to own this?
- How will it be reported on?
- Who will own this project?
- Who will the pilot group be?
- What will the success criteria for the pilot be?

14.5   The mind map

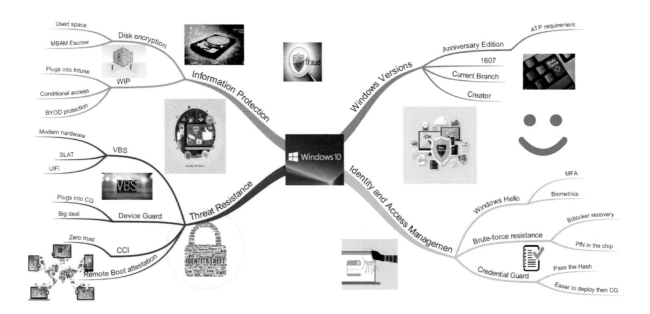

Notes:

15 PROTECT, DETECT& RESPOND – FEATURE MAPPING

The Microsoft security stance – Protect, Detect & Respond is a great starting point for this security journey, but what does what? You have already learned a little about each product so in this section, we are going to create three sections and fill them with the products so, that you can understand the balance. As you might expect here is a pretty heavy emphasis on "Protect".

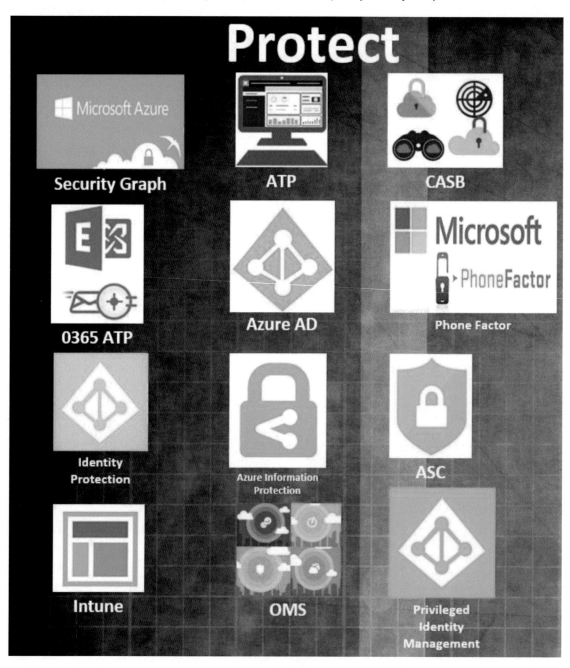

The "Detect" toolset features some overlap between the protect toolset, but some are standalone.

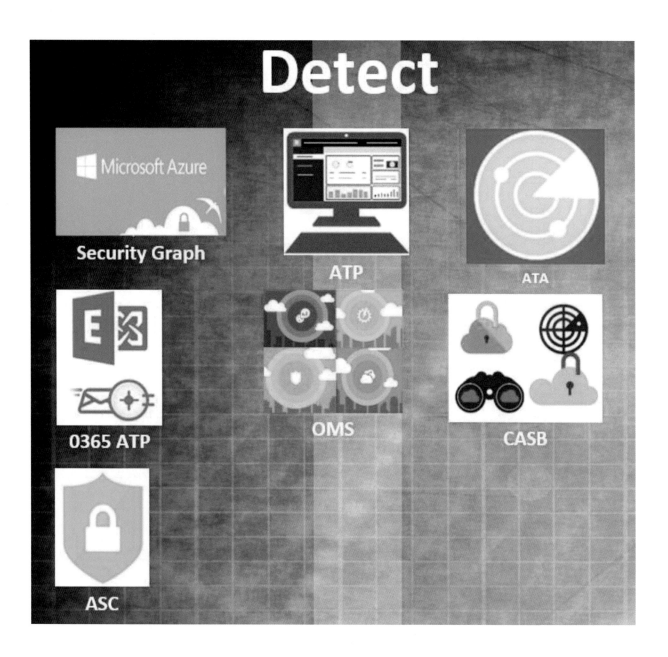

Lastly the response section of tools covers what tools can either be used to take action or will take action in an automated fashion.

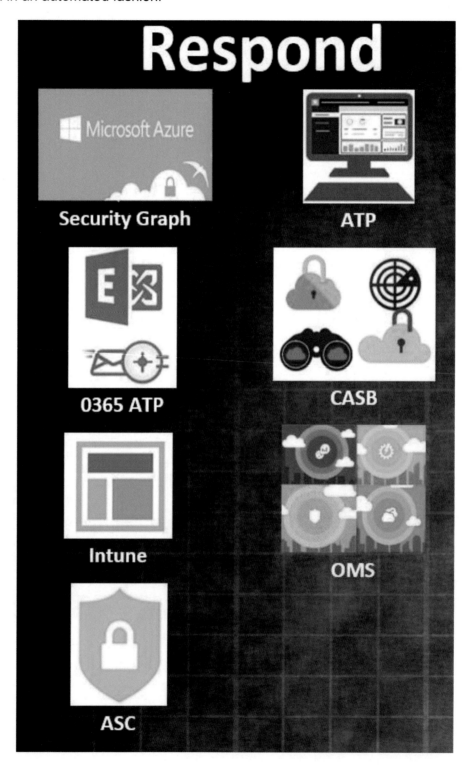

16 SEQUENCING THIS JOURNEY

There is so much to the new Microsoft security stance, where do we start? As a Solution Architect, I am asked this question all the time, and while a lot of this depends on so many factors, this is the roadmap that we default to, use this as a framework and then look to change as necessary.

As most of us have on-premises Active Directory, deploying ATA as your first step makes a lot of sense. Even if you have an existing intrusion detection system in place, trial this one out. The fact that it automatically connects to OMS brings the data to life. If you are a small "born in the cloud" company with no AD, then skip this.

Azure AD is the corner stone to the rest of this tool set, if you don't already have AAD in play (don't forget that if you are using O365 you already have AAD). You need to think about the several fundamental options around AAD. Even if you are not going to migrate to O365 the power of this suite comes from AAD.

Migrate to Windows 10. This is a big project for a lot of companies, so start it now. You have to protect the end point, doing so protects the user and data. Buy hardware that supports VBS, use secure boot, credential guard and Bitlocker everything.

ATP while not dependent on AAD we feel should come after AAD. ATP is such a powerful tool you will see results straight away, and feel a new sense of protection. You do need Windows 10, so if that is not your company standard then maybe consider that now too.

If you are already in O365 then O365 ATP is quick to deploy, has a great ROI and as its SaaS-based you will be up and going in no time. It's likely that if you do have O365, that maybe you went with some basic licensing and now is the time to consider some new additions.

In our experience now is the time to start your MFA project. There is a body of work getting everyone to register so why not start off with the IT and C-suite. It will serve you well for a number of the other projects to come.

With so many of the building blocks in place go ahead and enable and configure AAD-IP. This will help secure your cloud and in-house web based apps.

AAD-PIM will reduce the attack surface of your critical accounts and goes hand in hand with the last project. It's not hard to deploy and it's for a very specific user grouping of technical people so let's get this project in play now.

The OMS suite is both powerful and comprehensive. There are a lot of insights that this suite can bring from a security perspective so it makes sense to start on the log analytics parts now. This can be a pretty complex and detailed deployment so don't underestimate the effort.

Intune can really help your DLP/Azure Information Protection strategy so let's look at deploying Intune to your mobile estate. Any project that effects the end-point has the potential to cause issues so get the pilot going on this project now.

Azure Information Protection plays well with so many of the other tools and projects that have gone before this one. You need to consider the end user training component of this tool set.

Shadow IT can present a real challenge to modern secure information worker, so let's get the CASB into action and start protecting our O365 environment.

You will likely have more and more assets in Azure, and keeping them safe is the job of Azure Security Center. Get into this great tool now.

There are a lot of pieces to slot into this security framework so what are the resources you should consider?

Your Microsoft account team are always there to help and advise on what the best strategy is for you and your company. There are several ways to license all this technology, and you may find that you already own a lot of it.

A day in your local Microsoft Technology Center (MTC) is a great place to start; you can see this technology in action, kick the tires and ask questions on how it will work in your environment. The co-existence story is pretty key here. Microsoft has several Business Investing Funding (BIF) type programs that are designed to get you started with a number of these security drives.

Your Account Manager/Executive will likely want to start the conversation with your Account Technology Specialist. Between them, they will start to line up the conversations and demos you need with the different teams. Your local Microsoft partner that specializes in Azure security will be a great help and it's also quite likely that your account team may end up bringing us into the mix and we will be very happy to help wherever we can. This book will hopefully be the start of your security journey where identity is placed front and center in your approach to protecting your people, devices, and data, and I wish you well on that journey. You can email me direct from the QR code.

Best wishes

Paul Keely

paul@borninthecloud.net

AUTHORS

Paul Keely

Microsoft Most Valuable Professional (MVP)

Paul Keely is a 7 time's Microsoft MVP and runs his own consultancy practice. He has built a security solution accelerator called "The Secure Information Worker. He also works with large organizations to design and architect cloud based security projects. He is the founder of Born In the Cloud, a podcast and blog site centered around Azure topics. He speaks at Microsoft events throughout the world. When not working with Azure, he spends a lot of time skiing, running and climbing with his wife and two fantastic children.

Aman Sharma

Microsoft Most Valuable Professional (MVP)

Aman is one of only 8 Azure MVP's in Canada. He works as a principle technical consultant. His extensive developer background mixes well with his Azure IaaS experience to make him the perfect devops expert. Aman has a deep love of technology specifically cloud and cloud security.

Rob Kuehfus

Microsoft Cloud Solutions Architect (CSA)

Rob works at Microsoft as a CSA working with partners to build Azure consulting practices that lead the field. Rob was a Microsoft Program Manager from the System Center Product Group and Windows Product Group. Rob is someone who is passionate about technology and building out solutions that challenge him. When not deep in the technology weeds, he loves football (huge Hawks fan), working out and being proud father of 3 amazing kids.

Made in the USA
Columbia, SC
08 October 2020